Home Sweet Home

A Step-by-Step Guide for First Time Home Buyers

Empowering Tips, Strategies, and Check-lists to Simplify Your Path to Home-ownership.

This Book is NOT Just for First-Time Buyers!

Buying a home—whether it's your first or fifth—can feel overwhelming. This guide is packed with practical advice, checklists, and real-world strategies to help you avoid costly mistakes and navigate the process with confidence.

SALLY STREET

I0458829

Testimonials

From Overwhelmed to Overjoyed!

"Owning a home felt like an unattainable dream as I encountered one hurdle after another, leaving me increasingly perplexed. Thanks to the practical advice in this book, I am now delighted to call myself a homeowner."

Diana Beck

From Doubt to Keys in Hand,
The Credit Tips Changed My Life!

"I am in my 20s, and I never thought owning a home was possible. My credit score felt like a wall I couldn't climb, and I had no idea where to start. The credit tips in this book were life-changing—practical, easy to follow, and incredibly effective. In less than 45 days, I raised my score and qualified for a mortgage. Today, I'm standing in my own home! Words cannot describe the gratitude I feel for the advice in this book. It turned what seemed like an impossible dream into my new reality for our family."

Nic Garcia

Finding Home with Exceptional Guidance!

"Purchasing a home is a major commitment—one of life's most impactful decisions. Having the right people by your side is crucial. My connection with the author was undeniable; as the saying goes, you do business with people you like. As a realtor buying a home, this resonated deeply.

Her impact on our decision was profound, leaving us reassured we were on the right path to homeownership again. This experience reinforced the importance of treating every customer with respect and attention. Whether browsing or narrowing down options, everyone deserves equal care.

This story highlights the value of exceptional customer service in real estate, as noted by the National Association of Realtors. I'll carry this lesson throughout my career. Thank you for helping me find my dream home and teaching me through your example."

Brandy Olaniyan, Real Estate Agent

Got a Feedback Scan to Share!

Books That Brighten Your World!

ISBN: 978-1-967195-00-8 *Paperback*
ISBN: 978-1-967195-01-5 *Hardback*

Help Others Find Their Dream Home!

Thanks for continuing your journey with *Home Sweet Home*. If you have found value in this guide, sharing a quick review could help others take the leap toward homeownership. Your insights could **inspire someone else to make their dreams a reality.**

Making a difference is *easy!*

Just scan the QR code or click the link below to share your review:

https://a.co/d/62i4TOQ

Your effort to contribute to the conversation and share good vibes is deeply appreciated—thank you for creating an impact!

Thanks again, Sally Street

"THERE IS NO PLACE
LIKE HOME."

– L. FRANK BAUM

Home Sweet Home

Contents

Introduction

Welcome to Your Home-Buying Journey

Welcome to *Home Sweet Home: A Step-by-Step Guide for First-Time Home Buyers*! Congratulations—by picking up this book, you have already taken an exciting first step toward achieving one of life's biggest milestones: homeownership.

This guide was designed with first-time buyers in mind, but it is also packed with valuable insights, strategies, and checklists for anyone buying their next home. Whether you are just starting your journey or refining your search for your dream home, this book will be your trusted companion.

Home buying can be thrilling, but let's face it—it can also feel overwhelming. Do not worry! This guide will help you navigate the process, avoid common pitfalls, and make informed decisions that align with your goals. Together, we will take the mystery out of homeownership and turn your dream into a reality.

Why I Wrote This Book

For over 20 years, I have had the privilege of helping people navigate the home-buying process. During that time, I have witnessed the excitement, nervousness, and even the occasional panic that comes with this life-changing decision.

What inspired me to write this book? My passion for empowering people to make informed, confident decisions. I believe buying a home should be more exciting than intimidating, and I have seen firsthand how the proper guidance can make all the difference.

This book is my way of simplifying the complex steps of homeownership. By breaking the process into manageable pieces, I hope to give you the confidence and clarity you need to make this journey straightforward and successful.

Who This Book Is For

This guide is for anyone looking to buy a home, whether it is your first time or your next step. Are you a young professional dreaming of your first place? A newlywed couple starting your life together? A growing family in need of more space? This book is for you.

If terms like "escrow," "earnest money," or "contingencies" make your head spin, do not worry—you are not alone! This guide is written in plain language with relatable examples, practical strategies, and easy-to-follow checklists to make the process clear and manageable.

No matter where you are in your journey, this book will be your go-to resource for turning the dream of homeownership into a reality.

How You Will Benefit from This Book

Buying a home is not just a financial decision, it is a life-changing milestone. This guide is designed to make the process easier, smarter, and more enjoyable for you. Here is what you will gain:

- **Clarity**: A clear, step-by-step roadmap for navigating the home-buying process.

- **Confidence**: Practical advice that helps you understand what to expect and how to make informed choices.

- **Actionable Steps**: Checklists and tips to guide you through every stage of the journey.

- **Relatable Examples**: Real-world scenarios to make complex topics easier to understand.

- **Empowerment**: The tools and knowledge you need to make decisions that align with your financial and personal goals.

- **Glossary of Terms**: A comprehensive glossary at the end of the book to help you quickly understand any unfamiliar terms along the way.

Let's get started! Join me as we embark on this exciting journey toward homeownership.

Chapter 1

Should I Buy a Home?

Imagine walking through the door of your very own home—a space that is truly yours. It is an exciting thought, but is buying really better than renting? This chapter will help you weigh the pros and cons of homeownership to decide if it is the right step for you. Buying a home is a big decision, one of the biggest you will ever make. It is a bit like adopting a puppy: thrilling, slightly terrifying, and full of long-term commitment. Before jumping into the deep end, let's take a closer look at whether homeownership aligns with your goals and lifestyle.

The Pros of Buying a Home

Let's start on a positive note. Owning a home has many upsides, which is why so many people dream of it. Here are some of the major perks:

1. **Building Equity:** When you rent, your monthly payments are like giving someone a fistful of cash for the use of *their* property and waving goodbye to it forever. When you buy a home, your payments help build equity—the portion of the property you truly own, free from any liens. Think of it as a savings account that has the potential to grow over time. Think of it like a savings account that could grow over time.

   a. What is Equity? Equity is the portion of a property's value that you truly own. It is calculated as the difference between the property's market value and the remaining balance on any loans secured by the property. **Example:** If your home is worth $300,000 and you owe $200,000 on your mortgage, your equity is $100,000.

2. **Stability & Control:** No more random rent increases or surprise notices about moving out. You call the shots. Want to paint your walls lime green or adopt a Great Dane? Go for it!

3. **Long-Term Investment:** Historically, real estate tends to appreciate over time. While there are no guarantees, owning a home can be a smart way to build wealth over time.

4. **Potential Tax Breaks:** You could be eligible for tax deductions on mortgage interest and property taxes, depending on your circumstances. That is like finding money under your couch cushions—only better.

5. **Sense of Community:** Owning a home typically deepens your connection to your neighborhood. It is where you live and where you plant roots, form relationships, and become part of a community. From waving to neighbors and helping each other to joining local events, homeownership turns a collection of houses into a place where you truly belong.

The Cons of Buying a Home

But it is not all sunshine and white picket fences. Owning a home comes with challenges, too:

1. **Upfront Costs:** The down payment, closing costs, inspections, and moving expenses add up fast. It is not small change, so you must be financially prepared.

2. **Maintenance and Repairs:** When the toilet breaks or the roof leaks, there is no landlord to call. You will be doing your own lawn care. You are the one fixing it (or hiring

someone to do it), and that is an ongoing cost of homeownership.

3. **Less Flexibility:** Want to move across the country for an incredible new job? Selling a home takes time and effort, unlike breaking a lease, which often requires some paperwork and small fees. However, be cautious— breaking a lease can impact your credit if not appropriately handled. Speak with your landlord to understand the terms of your lease, as you may face a two-month penalty or, in some cases, be required to pay out the remaining duration of the lease. Clear communication and careful planning can help you avoid any surprises or credit dings.

4. **Market Fluctuations:** The value of your home could go up—or down. While buying is generally a sound long-term investment, the market can be unpredictable in the short term.

5. **Hidden Costs:** It is not just the mortgage payment that you will need to budget for. You will also need to budget for property taxes, homeowners insurance, Homeowners Association (HOA) fees, and the occasional surprise repair.

What is an HOA?

A **Homeowners Association (HOA)** is an organization that manages and enforces rules for a residential community, such as a single-family neighborhood, condominium complex, or townhouse development. HOAs are typically governed by a board of residents and funded by monthly or annual fees paid by homeowners.

HOAs handle tasks like maintaining common areas (e.g., parks, pools, or landscaping), enforcing community rules (e.g., property appearance or noise restrictions), and sometimes managing shared services like trash collection or security. Their goal is to preserve property values and foster a cohesive community, but their rules and fees can vary significantly. Be sure to ask questions and review a copy of the HOA rules before committing to a property.

Renting vs. Owning: A Quick Comparison

Now, let's compare renting and owning head-to-head. After all, the alternative to buying is continuing to rent, and both options have their merits.

Benefits of Renting

- **Flexibility**: Easy to relocate when a new opportunity arises.

- **Lower Maintenance**: No lawnmowers or leaking faucets to worry about.

- **Predictable Expenses**: Rent is usually a fixed amount, with fewer surprises.

Downsides of Renting

- **No Equity**: You are paying someone else's mortgage.

- **Lack of Control**: Want a pet or to hang art on the wall? Better check the lease.
- **Rent Increases**: Landlords can increase rent, sometimes significantly, and enforce additional policies.

Benefits of Owning

- **Long-Term Investment**: Potential for owner appreciation and wealth-building.
- **Creative Freedom**: Decorate, remodel, or plant a garden.
- **Stability**: Consistent monthly payments with a fixed-rate mortgage.

Downsides of Owning

- **Upfront Costs**: Higher initial investment.
- **Ongoing Maintenance**: Responsibility for upkeep and repairs.
- **Market Risk**: Property values can fluctuate.

Renting vs. Owning

Renting can feel a bit like tossing your hard-earned money into a trash can. You know it is gone, but you are not quite sure where it went. Buying a home, on the other hand, is like planting a money tree in your own yard. With every mortgage payment, you are not just paying for a roof over your head and the land it sits on; you are building equity and growing your wealth. Rising home values often mean your money tree gets taller and stronger over time. Sure, you cannot always predict the market, but wouldn't you rather grow your money than watch it disappear?

Real-Life Scenario: "Is Buying Right for Me?"

Meet Helen and Aaron. They are a young couple renting a cozy apartment in a trendy neighborhood. They love the convenience and have even grown fond of their landlord's cat, Mittens. But they are feeling cramped, and their landlord just announced a rent increase. So, they are considering buying.

What is holding them back?

Helen and Aaron are worried about the financial commitment, the cost of repairs, and how it might limit their job flexibility. But they are also tempted by the idea of building equity and having more space. After reviewing their budget, they decided to start looking for a starter home—something modest that fits their budget.

Key Takeaway: There is no perfect answer—only what is best for you. The scales tipped toward buying for Helen and Aaron, but that does not mean it is right for everyone. You must weigh the pros and cons and decide what works for your situation.

Real-Life Scenario: "Should I Wait to Buy?"

Meet David. He is a 32-year-old marketing professional renting a spacious apartment downtown. David loves his current setup—it offers excellent amenities, a short commute to work, and plenty of nearby restaurants to explore. However, he has been hearing a lot about the benefits of homeownership, and he is feeling the pressure to buy.

What is holding him back?

David's job might transfer him to another city within the following year. While he is tempted by the idea of building equity and owning a place to call his own, he knows the uncertainty of his career plans could make buying a risky move. After considering the financial and logistical challenges of selling or renting out a home in a new city, he decides to hold off for now.

Key Takeaway: Timing is everything when it comes to buying a home. For David, the possibility of relocating soon means it is wiser to wait and maintain flexibility. Before jumping into homeownership, make sure your personal and professional plans align with the long-term commitment of buying a home.

Top Mistakes to Avoid When Deciding to Buy

- **Not Reviewing Your Finances**: Thoroughly examine your savings, debts, and monthly budget. If it feels like a stretch, ask yourself: Is this just a fear of change, or is it realistically within your means without overextending yourself? (Just because you qualify for a larger loan does not mean it is right for you.)

- **Rushing the Process**: Take your time. Buying a home is a marathon, not a sprint. However, overanalyzing can cause commitment or decision-making paralysis and may keep you renting forever.

- **Ignoring the Total Cost**: The mortgage is not the only cost; consider taxes, insurance, and upkeep, too.

- **Buying Based on Emotion**: It is easy to fall in love with a home, but make sure it fits your budget and needs.

- **Overlooking Resale Value**: Even if it is your dream home now, think about how easy (or hard) it might be to sell later.

Helpful Hint - Get Pre-Qualified NOW!

Whether you are confident you are ready to buy a home or just starting to think about it, remember that knowledge is power. Understanding where you stand financially and what you can afford is a crucial first step. A winning strategy is to get prequalified for a mortgage NOW! This simple step not only shows you what is possible now but also helps you plan for the future if you are not quite ready yet. Knowing your budget, borrowing potential, and what lenders are looking for can provide a clear path forward, empowering you to take confident steps toward homeownership—whether today, tomorrow, or a few years down the road. More details about getting prequalified and how lenders look at things come later in the book.

For now, just know prequalification is the essential FIRST action item!

Thoughts to Consider

At the end of the day, deciding whether to buy a home is deeply personal. It is okay if you are not ready right now—there is no rule that says you have to own a home to be successful or happy. If buying makes sense financially, logistically, and emotionally, then go for it. If not, renting can be a wise and strategic choice until the time is right.

So, take a deep breath, grab a cup of coffee, and consider your options carefully. Whether you buy or continue renting, be confident that you are taking a step toward a better future. And that is something worth celebrating, maybe with a spa day or with a good pizza on the couch.

The Cost of Waiting: Sam's Lesson in Lost Wealth

Let's talk about Sam. Sam is a young professional who spent years renting in a bustling city where apartments were easy to find, but privacy and control were a different story. Like many of us, Sam wanted the flexibility and low commitment that renting offered—no leaky faucets to fix, no lawns to mow, and the freedom to move if life took an unexpected turn. But Sam also had a nagging thought in the back of his mind: **Should I buy a home?**

Sam had a good job, a decent savings account, and was building a stable life, but the idea of homeownership felt daunting. The thought of a mortgage payment, property taxes, and maintenance gave him pause. And so, he continued renting, figuring he would buy when he was "really ready."

The Missed Opportunity

A few years ago, Sam considered buying a two-bedroom condo in a neighborhood he loved. The unit was listed at $300,000 then, and the mortgage would have been affordable. But he decided to wait, feeling he "was not quite ready." Fast-forward to today and that same condo is now valued at $445,000. Rents, too, have increased, and his rent has increased significantly in the last few years.

By choosing to rent, Sam missed the opportunity to build equity in that condo and faced rising rent without any control over future increases. In effect, Sam was helping his landlord build wealth while his net worth stayed the same—or even decreased, considering inflation and rising rent costs.

How Buying Could Have Built Wealth

If Sam had bought that condo at $300,000, he would have had the chance to build something real—**equity**. Equity is the value of your ownership in a property, and it grows as you pay down your mortgage and as the home's value appreciates. For instance:

- Let's say Sam puts down 5% ($15,000) on the condo and finances the remaining $285,000.

- His mortgage payments would have partially gone toward reducing the loan balance, while also covering the interest, as the condo's value increased.

- Fast-forward to today. With the condo valued at $445,000, Sam would have gained $145,000 in equity, not including the amount he paid down on the mortgage.

That $145,000 could be put toward a down payment on a larger home, invested, saved for a rainy day, or just allowed it to keep growing toward his retirement plan. By not buying, Sam missed out on this valuable growth opportunity.

The Cost of Renting vs. Buying

While renting is flexible and does not require a down payment, it also does not offer any return on the money spent. Renting feels like you are paying a mortgage—just not your own. As property values rise, rent increases frequently follow, meaning tenants may pay more over time without gaining any financial return.

If Sam had put those monthly payments toward his mortgage instead, he would have been building equity with each payment, and his monthly payment would likely have remained stable. **The lesson?** Renting can be an ongoing expense that builds your landlord's wealth rather than your own.

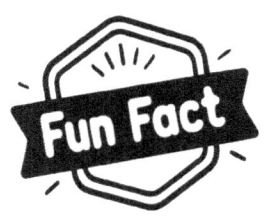

Fun Fact: The long-term cost of paying rent can be truly eye-opening. Take a look at the chart based on your current monthly rent. For example, if you are paying $2,500 a month in rent over 10 years, that adds up to a staggering $300,000. Surprising, isn't it? Imagine if that money or at least a portion of it was building your future instead of contributing to your landlord's wealth.

Cost of Paying Rent Over Time

RENT	5 YRS	10 YRS	15 YRS	20 YRS	25 YRS	30 YRS
$1K	$60K	$120K	$180K	$240K	$300K	$360K
$1.5K	$90K	$180K	$270K	$360K	$450K	$540K
$2K	$120K	$240K	$360K	$480K	$600K	$720K
$2.5K	$150K	$300K	$450K	$600K	$750K	$900K
$3K	$180K	$360K	$540K	$720K	$900K	$1.080M
$3.5K	$210K	$420K	$630K	$840K	$1.050M	$1.260M
$4K	$240K	$480K	$720K	$960K	$1.200M	$1.440M
$4.5K	$270K	$540K	$810K	$1.080M	$1.350M	$1.620M
$5K	$300K	$600K	$900K	$1.200M	$1.500M	$1.800M
$5.5K	$330K	$660K	$990K	$1.320M	$1.650M	$1.980M
$6K	$360K	$720K	$1.080M	$1.440M	$1.800M	$2.160M

Realizing the Financial Benefits of Homeownership: So, why do people like Sam hesitate to buy even when they are financially ready? Often, it is fear of commitment, concern about maintenance, or not knowing where to start. But let's look at some of the significant benefits Sam would have gained by making the jump into homeownership:

1. **Appreciation**: Real estate typically increases in value over time. Even at a modest appreciation rate, homes tend to be worth more over the long haul. In our scenario, Sam would have seen his condo appreciate $145,000, giving him a nice increase in net worth.

2. **Stability**: Homeownership provides predictability. While rents, insurance, and taxes can rise with market trends, a fixed-rate mortgage stays stable, providing a long-term financial anchor.

3. **Wealth-Building Tool**: Sam would have been creating a sort of forced savings by paying down the mortgage. Each payment would have brought him closer to fully owning a valuable asset.

4. **Tax Benefits**: Homeowners often benefit from tax deductions on mortgage interest and property taxes. These breaks can add up, making homeownership even more financially attractive.

Top Mistakes to Avoid: Sam's story illustrates a few common mistakes that many first-time buyers make:

- **Waiting for the "Perfect Time"**: If you can afford to buy, waiting might mean missing out on years of appreciation and equity. The "perfect time" rarely comes.

- **Not Weighing the Cost of Renting**: While renting may seem cheaper initially, consider that you are building your landlord's wealth instead of your own. Do your math.

- **Letting Fear Drive Decisions**: Fear of maintenance, the unknowns of homeownership, or market fluctuations can hold you back. But remember, there is a whole industry of professionals—agents, inspectors, attorneys, lenders—who are there to help you.

Chapter 1 Key Takeaways

1. **Consider the Long-Term Financial Impact**: Renting may seem convenient, but you may give up long-term wealth-building potential if you can afford to buy.

2. **Do not Let Rising Prices Intimidate You**: Real estate values generally trend upward. Waiting for prices to go down often means you could be paying more in the future.

3. **Homeownership Is a Financial Investment**: It is not just about a place to live; it is about building equity, stability, and a sense of ownership.

4. **Know When You are Ready**: Assess your finances honestly. If you are financially prepared, consider taking the leap, as the long-term rewards often outweigh the initial costs.

Summary: If Sam had bought that condo, he would be sitting on a comfortable $145,000 increase in value, plus any equity from his mortgage payments. Instead, he is faced with a higher rent payment and regretting a missed financial opportunity. Homeownership can be one of the best tools for building wealth, providing stability, and turning what feels like an endless stream of rent payments into something meaningful.

If you are unsure about buying a home and there is no strong reason holding you back, consider Sam's story as a reminder of what is possible. If you are financially ready, take the leap and begin investing in your future through homeownership. Next up, let's look at what to prioritize when searching for your dream home.

"YOUR BIGGEST FINANCIAL MISTAKE WAS NOT BUYING A HOME AT THE AGE OF 5."

- DAVE RAMSEY

Home Sweet Home

Chapter 2

Your Home-Hunting Adventure Begins

Congratulations! You have decided to embark on one of life's most exciting journeys: finding your next home sweet home. Whether this is your first time buying or you are upgrading to your next dream home, the process is filled with possibilities—and, to be honest, a few challenges.

This chapter will help you clarify your priorities, avoid common pitfalls, and stay focused on what matters most to you. Think of it as your road map to finding a home that feels just right—like your first sip of morning coffee, but better.

Step 1: How Long Do You Plan to Stay? Start by asking yourself one of the most critical questions: *How long do I plan to live in this home?* This is not just about imagining your future; it is about aligning your decision with your timeline.

- **Short-Term Buyers (Under 5 Years)**:

  If you plan to move in a few years, focus on resale potential. Choose a home in a desirable location with low-maintenance features that appeal to many buyers. Do not forget to factor in market trends—buying in a rapidly appreciating area could mean a higher return when you sell. Prioritize **affordability** so you are not stretched too thin financially.

- **Long-Term Buyers (10+ Years)**:

  For those putting down roots, consider how the home and neighborhood will grow with you. Will it accommodate future needs, like starting a family or working remotely? Look at factors like schools, commute times, and room for potential expansions.

Tip: Whether short- or long-term, think about how the home fits your lifestyle now and how it might evolve.

Step 2: How Many Bedrooms & Square Footage? These are two of the most common filters used in any online home search—and for good reason. Property size can help determine how well a home fits your current and future needs.

- **Number of Bedrooms**: Ask yourself how many bedrooms you *really* need. For example:
  - Are you living alone or with a partner?
  - Do you plan to expand your family in the next few years?
  - Would a guest room or home office improve your lifestyle?
- **Square Footage**: Square footage is not just a number—it is your personal space budget.
  - Love entertaining? You might need extra space.
  - Want to keep costs down? Remember, more square footage often means higher utility bills and maintenance.
  - Focus on the layout over the size. A well-designed 1,200-square-foot home can feel more spacious than a poorly designed 1,500-square-foot one.

- **Step 3: Needs vs. Wants—Sorting It All Out:** You have probably started a mental list of "must-haves" and "nice-to-haves." Let's put it on paper and make it official.

- **Needs (Non-Negotiables)**:
  These are deal-breakers. A home without them simply will not work. Examples include:
    - Location close to work or family
    - A safe neighborhood
    - A minimum number of bedrooms and bathrooms
    - Staying within your budget

- **Wants (Nice-to-Haves)**: These are things that would be great but are not essential. Examples include:
    - Fancy countertops
    - A swimming pool
    - Extra-large backyard

Real-Life Scenario: Sorting Needs from Wants

Meet John, a single professional who is tired of renting. He is set on buying a two-bedroom condo near his office. He thinks he needs a gym in the building, a balcony, and top-of-the-line appliances. But when he starts touring condos, he realizes the ones with these features are way out of his budget.

He takes a step back, revisits his list, and distinguishes his **real needs** (proximity to work, two bedrooms, good natural light) from his **wants** (the gym and balcony). Jake eventually finds a condo that meets his needs and has one of his wants—a small patio. He is thrilled!

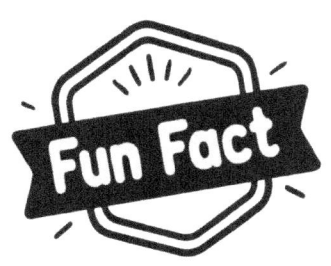 **Fun Fact:** most buyers change their minds about what they want. Maybe you start dead-set on a single-story ranch but fall in love with a charming two-story colonial. Or you are convinced you want to be in a bustling downtown area but discover a hidden gem in a quieter suburb.

Key Takeaway: You will find a satisfying and sensible home by being realistic about your needs and wants. Also, get pre-qualified FIRST so that you are confident that you are looking at homes within your desired budget.

Changing your mind is entirely normal! House hunting is a process, and your perspective will likely shift as you see more homes. So, do not stress about getting it "right" from day one—be open to exploring different options.

Step 4: Finding the Right Area and Neighborhood: The location of your home is just as important as the layout. The right neighborhood should align with your lifestyle and daily needs, so take time to think about what matters most to you.

Key Factors to Consider:

- **Commute**: How far are you willing to drive to work, school, or your favorite coffee shop? Factor in traffic patterns during rush hours and what that commute will look like day-to-day.

- **Amenities**: Look for nearby parks, nature trails, shopping centers, entertainment, and public transportation options that suit your lifestyle.

- **Vibe**: Do you prefer a bustling city vibe, a quiet suburb, or a rural retreat?

- **Safety**: Check online crime rates and drive through the neighborhood at different times of the day to get a feel for the area, as well as the traffic volume on the street.

- **Schools:** While living in a good school district can boost the value of your property and appeal to future buyers, it is not the only factor that adds value. Other neighborhood features, such as being near a lake, a golf course, vibrant entertainment options, or unique amenities, can also significantly enhance a home's desirability.

It is helpful to explore neighborhoods in person. Spend a weekend driving around, visiting local spots, and picturing yourself living there.

Visualizing Your Ideal Areas: Use a map—physical or digital—and mark the areas you would consider living in. If your goal is to stay within a 40-minute drive of a specific location, draw a circle with that radius around your key spot. This is an easy and practical way to narrow your focus. Not sure where to begin? Start by identifying places that matter most to you, such as your workplace, family, or favorite hangouts.

If you are uncertain about specific neighborhoods, that is okay! Start by identifying a general radius around your key destinations. As you learn more about different areas, you can refine your search.

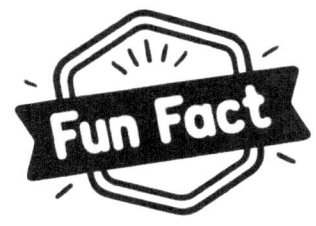

Fun Fact: Some buyers introduce themselves to potential neighbors before making an offer. It is not a bad idea—you will be living next to them, so it is helpful to get a sense of the community vibe before you commit!

Step 5: Your Lifestyle Needs: Home Type Matters: The type of home you choose should align with your lifestyle, priorities, and long-term goals. Are you looking for low-maintenance living, room for a growing family, or a unique space to call your own? Your preferences for upkeep, privacy, and functionality will help guide this decision. Below, we break down common home types and how they fit different lifestyles.

Types of Homes

- **Townhouse or Condo**: Great for low-maintenance living. You will have less yard work and often share maintenance costs with other owners. If you travel a lot or are just looking for a second home for a few months a year, these usually offer a "lock and leave" lifestyle. However, you will also have less privacy.

- **Duplex:** Often more affordable, you can buy one unit or the whole duplex and rent the other side out, which can help you reach your equity goals faster.

- **Single-Family Pre-Owned Home**: Offers more space, privacy, and often a yard. But be prepared for more maintenance and higher utility bills.

- **Ranch or One-Level Living**: Ideal for those who prefer no stairs and easy accessibility.

- **Fixer-Upper**: If you are handy (or have a good contractor), a fixer-upper can be a cost-effective way to customize a home to your liking.

- **New Home**: Brand-new homes often feature modern designs, energy-efficient features, lower utility bills, and updated appliances. They typically require less immediate maintenance and usually include builder warranties for added peace of mind.

- **Manufactured or Mobile Home**: A budget-friendly option that provides flexibility and affordability. While these homes might have fewer customization options, they can be an excellent choice for those seeking a more cost-effective way to own property.

- **Tiny Home**: Ideal for minimalists or those looking to downsize, tiny homes offer affordability, low maintenance, and a smaller ecological footprint.

- **Custom-Built Home**: This option is Ideal for those who want complete control over the design of their home, layout, and features. While more expensive upfront, it ensures the house fits your exact needs and preferences.

- **Multi-Family Property**: This category includes triplexes or fourplexes, which are great for investors or those looking to live in one unit and rent out the others to generate income and build equity.

- **Cottage or Cabin**: Often, smaller and cozy cottages and cabins are ideal for vacation homes or those looking for charm and character in a rural setting.

Conclusion: Choosing the right home type is about finding the balance between your lifestyle, budget, and long-term goals. Whether you are drawn to the low-maintenance appeal of a condo, the customization potential of a fixer-upper, or the investment opportunities of a multi-family property, understanding the pros and cons of each option will help you make an informed decision. Take the time to assess your needs, and you will find the home that best suits your unique way of life.

Step 6: New or Used? Choosing the Right Fit for Your Lifestyle: Here is the truth: no home is perfect. Every house has quirks—whether it is a tiny bathroom, a dated kitchen, or a squeaky floorboard. Instead of chasing perfection, focus on how the potential home offers to meet your needs and become the space you envision over time.

Tips for Keeping an Open Mind

- **Prioritize Essentials**: Identify your must-haves and be flexible about your wants. A home does not need to check every box to be a great fit.

- **Look Beyond Cosmetics**: Paint colors, wallpaper, and light fixtures are easy to update. Focus on the structure and layout instead.

- **Think About Upgrades Over Time**: Small renovations done gradually can transform a home without overwhelming your budget.

New vs. Used Homes: What is Right for You?

The choice between a new or used home can significantly shape your experience. Here are the pros and cons of each option:

New Homes

- **Move-In Ready**: Brand new and up to code, offering a hassle-free start.

- **Minimal Repairs**: Lower maintenance costs in the early years.

- **Customizable Options**: If purchased before construction is complete, you can often choose finishes and upgrades.

- **Builder Warranties**: Most new homes come with warranties covering major systems, appliances, and structural elements for a set period. This added peace of mind can save you significant repair costs during the early years of homeownership.

Used Homes

- **More Character**: Older homes often have unique charm and distinctive features.

- **Established Neighborhoods**: Mature neighborhoods may offer larger trees, defined community spaces, and more amenities.

- **Affordability**: Older homes typically cost less per square foot.

- **Limited Warranties**: Unlike new homes, used homes do not typically come with builder warranties. However, you can negotiate a home warranty into the sale, which can cover certain repairs or replacements for appliances and systems during the first year of ownership.

If you are considering a used home, think about potential renovation needs. A fixer-upper can be a cost-effective way to personalize a property, but it is important to know what you are getting into.

Pro Insight: Before committing, make a detailed list of repairs or updates and obtain quotes from contractors. For example, replacing a roof might be manageable, but a full kitchen remodel could stretch your budget.

"START SMALL AND WORK YOUR WAY UP."

– SAM DOGEN

Home Sweet Home

Chapter 2 Key Takeaways

- **No Perfect Home**: Embrace the quirks and focus on a home's potential to meet your needs.

- **New vs. Used Homes:** New homes offer modern amenities and warranties, while used homes may provide character and affordability.

- **Realtor Guidance**: Whether buying new or used, a Realtor can offer valuable expertise, advocacy, and negotiation skills to help you get the best value.

- **Think Long-Term**: Small updates and gradual improvements can transform any home into your dream space over time.

Summary: Finding the right area, neighborhood, and home type is just as crucial as choosing the perfect layout. This chapter explores the key factors to consider, from commute times and safety to lifestyle needs and long-term goals. It provides practical tools like mapping your ideal locations and evaluating home types to ensure they align with your priorities. Additionally, it outlines the pros and cons of new and used homes, emphasizing flexibility and focusing on a home's potential rather than perfection.

Let's shift gears and discuss avoiding miscommunication and how it is key to a smooth process to get everyone aligned.

Chapter 3

Avoiding Miscommunication: The Scale of 1-10

Feeling overwhelmed by the choices? Try this simple trick: rate each feature on a scale from 1 to 10, where 10 is "must-have," 5 is not a big deal either way, and 1 is "not important at all."

Example:

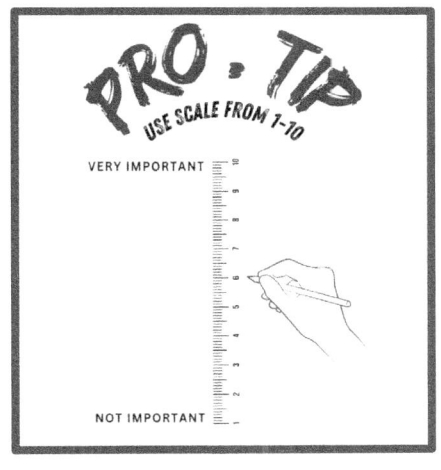

- A home office for remote work might be a 9 or 10 if it is essential to your daily routine.

- A swimming pool might be a 3 or 5—nice to have but not a deal-breaker.

Tip: Ask each decision-maker to create their own list independently, then compare the results. This approach encourages meaningful conversations and ensures that everyone's preferences are acknowledged. For example, if one partner rates having a game room as an 8 (a strong preference) and the other rates it as 5 (indifferent), the average score would be 6.5. This might lead you to explore a mix of homes, some with game rooms and some without. After viewing a few options, you can re-score and regroup, reevaluate your priorities, and refine your search to create a more focused vision for the next round of house hunting.

Real-Life Scenario: Avoiding Miscommunication

John insisted he wanted a corner lot, so his wife Lisa and their agent focused their search exclusively on homes with that feature. However, after weeks of frustration and limited options, John admitted the corner lot was only a "5" on his priority scale—it was not essential. His real priority? A spacious kitchen. Once they shifted focus, they quickly found their dream home.

From Overwhelmed to Aligned:
The 1-10 Decision Framework

Clear communication with other decision-makers is critical when searching for the ideal home. Aligned priorities and honest discussions can make the process much smoother and more productive. A memorable experience with John and Lisa highlights how the 1-10 method can prevent miscommunication and ensure the search stays on track.

From the outset, John frequently mentioned his desire for a corner lot, and his repeated emphasis led Lisa and their agent to focus solely on homes with that feature. This narrowed their options significantly, making it challenging to find homes that met their other essential criteria.

After several weeks of limited progress, the agent asked John, "On a scale of 1 to 10, how important is having a corner lot to you?" To everyone's surprise, he rated it a 5. When the agent asked why he had mentioned it so often, John explained, "I thought corner lots might provide more space and privacy, but it is not a deal-breaker. It was just something my dad always recommended. What we really need is a spacious kitchen and a layout that fits our lifestyle."

This realization was a turning point. By shifting the focus to their true priorities, the agent helped to expand their search and quickly found a home that met all their essential needs, even though it was not on a corner lot. It turned out to be the ideal fit for them.

Lesson Learned: It is essential to focus on what truly matters to your needs and lifestyle—not on someone else's preferences or assumptions.

Everyday Life Tip: The Versatility of the 1-10 Method

Using a scale of 1-10 is not just helpful for house hunting—it is an excellent tool for daily communication. Whether rating how much you enjoyed a meal, deciding whether to attend a concert or planning where to go on vacation, this method gives clarity and context. Instead of vague responses like "It is fine," assigning a number helps others understand the intensity or importance of your preferences.

This approach fosters open dialogue, reduces misunderstandings, and speeds up decision-making—whether you are choosing a movie or debating what to do this weekend!

The 1-10 Life Hack: Faster, Clearer, Better Decisions

Feeling overwhelmed by too many options? Try using the scale of 1-10 to simplify decision-making. Rate each item on your house-hunting list to help prioritize what matters most.

- **10**: A must-have; you wouldn't consider a home without it.

- **5**: Neutral; it is nice but not a big deal either way.

- **1**: Actively undesirable.

If one partner rates a feature as a 10 and the other gives it a 5, it is worth discussing its importance and finding common ground. This method helps ensure everyone's preferences are considered and can guide you toward the best-fit home.

Your House Hunting Checklist Scale of 1-10: Reminder: Each decision-maker should fill this out individually. Circle the item that best suits you and rate it. Once completed, compare your answers, discuss your priorities, and align on the bottom line for your group's shared priorities and scale rankings.

	Home Buying Checklist	Rate 1-10	Notes (if you want to expound on your thoughts)
Home Type	Townhouse, Condo, Duplex, Single-Family Home etc.		
	New Homes, Pre-owned, Fixer-upper		

	Home Buying Checklist	Rate 1-10	Notes (if you want to expound on your thoughts)
Storage & Practicality	Storage space (closets, attic, basement)		
	Garage or parking availability		
	Storage for recreational items (bikes, boats, etc.)		
	Storage for seasonal decorations		
	Size of laundry room or location		

Scan to download editable & printable format.

	Home Buying Checklist	Rate 1-10	Notes (if you want to expound on your thoughts)
Property Features	Number of bedrooms		
	Number of bathrooms		
	Other Rooms: (game room, media, formal areas, etc.)		
	1, 2 or 3 story home		
	Fireplace		
	Overall square footage range		
	Kitchen size and layout		
	Ceiling height		
	Floor plan layout and flow		
	Room for future expansion		
	Home style or architectural design		
	Yard size		
	Outdoor space for entertaining		
	Curb appeal (or is the inside or location more important)		
	View		

	Home Buying Checklist	Rate 1-10	Notes (if you want to expound on your thoughts)
Location	Location		
	Proximity to work		
	Proximity to family and friends		
	Access to public transportation		
	Walkability of the neighborhood		
	Neighborhood safety		
	School district quality		
	Commuter traffic patterns (and alternative routes)		

	Home Buying Checklist	Rate 1-10	Notes (if you want to expound on your thoughts)
Technology & Connectivity	Internet and cell service quality		
	Availability of home office space		

	Home Buying Checklist	Rate 1-10	Notes (if you want to expound on your thoughts)
Condition & Maintenance: (If you are only looking at New Homes, you can skip this section)	Condition of the roof		
	Age and condition of major systems (HVAC, plumbing, electrical)		
	Energy efficiency		
	Move-in readiness		
	Potential for renovations or upgrades		
	Water pressure and plumbing quality		
	Quality of appliances (if included)		

	Home Buying Checklist	Rate 1-10	Notes (if you want to expound on your thoughts)
Financial Conside-rations	Price and affordability		
	Local taxes and utility costs		
	Flood zone or natural disaster risks		
	Future resale value		
	Zoning laws or future developments in the area		

	Home Buying Checklist	Rate 1-10	Notes (if you want to expound on your thoughts)
Comm-unity & Amenities	Community amenities (pools, parks, gyms)		
	Lock & Leave lifestyle		
	Nearby shopping and dining options		
	Proximity to healthcare facilities		
	Accessibility for individuals with mobility needs		
	Availability of recycling and trash services		
	Homeowners Association (HOA) fees or restrictions		

	Home Buying Checklist	Rate 1-10	Notes (if you want to expound on your thoughts)
Other (add your checklists here)			

46

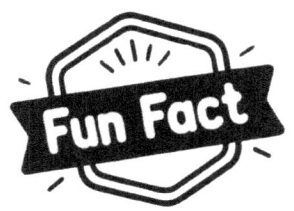

Fun Fact: Homes near parks and green spaces tend to have higher resale values.

Chapter 3 Key Takeaways

- **Clarify Priorities**: Use the 1-10 scale to identify what matters most and communicate openly with decision-makers.

- **Avoid Assumptions**: Do not rely solely on repeated mentions of a feature—ask why it is important and how it fits your lifestyle.

- **Embrace Flexibility**: Be open to reevaluating and refining priorities as you explore homes.

- **Focus on Essentials**: Remember that no home will have everything, but the right one will meet your most important needs.

- **Keep the Big Picture in Mind**: Finding the right home is about creating a place that fits your life and future, not about checking every box on your wish list.

Summary: Finding the right home is more than just bricks and mortar—it is about creating a space that works for your life. Be open, stay true to your priorities, and enjoy the process. You will know the right home when you find it—just like stumbling upon a secret stash of your favorite chocolate!

You have clarified your priorities—now it is time to figure out how to make a winning offer.

Chapter 4

Once I Find a Home, How Do I Know What to Offer?

You have found a home that feels like "the one"—the kind of place that makes your heart race and your imagination run wild. Now comes one of the most crucial steps in the homebuying journey: deciding how much to offer. Think of it like a strategic game—you will need to balance your excitement with careful planning while keeping some cards close to your chest. This chapter will guide you through the process of crafting a competitive yet fair offer. If any terms or concepts seem unclear, remember to check the glossary at the end of the book for quick explanations. Once you master this step, you will be ready to move forward with confidence.

Understanding Fair Market Value: What is the House Really Worth?

Before deciding on an offer, it is essential to determine the home's fair market value, essentially, what the property is worth in today's market. In real estate, there is a saying that sums it up: the three most important factors in determining a property's value are location, location, and location.

Fair market value is determined by several factors:

- **Location**: If you are in a major metropolitan area, what is the distance to downtown? Even if you do not work or go downtown, this is important to a high percentage of home buyers, so this can affect how much and how quickly your home might go up in value.

- **Location**: What is the distance to jobs, shopping, hospitals, schools, and restaurants?

- **Location**: A prime spot boosts the home's value, while a less desirable location might bring it down. Prime could mean it is a reasonable distance to downtown, as mentioned, but it could also mean that it is near a lake, entertainment, attractions, outdoor activities,

- **Condition**: Is the home in move-in condition, or does it need minor or major repairs?

- **Comparable Sales (Comps)**: Your Real Estate agent can provide these for you and go over them with you. These are recent sales of similar homes in the area, and they are your best clue about a fair offer. It is important to remember that a house can be listed for any price, meaning some homes on the market might be overpriced. When reviewing "comps," focus on properties that have sold and officially closed to get an accurate comparison.

Seller's Disclosure: What You Need to Know

A seller's disclosure is a document provided by the seller that outlines any known issues or defects with the property. It is a valuable tool for buyers to understand the home's condition beyond what meets the eye. The disclosure might include details about past repairs, ongoing maintenance concerns, or potential problems like water damage, foundation issues, or electrical faults.

In most cases, you will receive the seller's disclosure before making an offer. Reviewing this document carefully can help you decide whether to proceed, request additional inspections, or negotiate repairs or concessions. However, not all states require sellers to provide a disclosure. If the seller fails to provide one as required or if something on the disclosure raises concerns, you may have the right to terminate the sale, depending on the laws in your area and the terms of your contract. Your agent can guide you on the best course of action.

Earnest Money:

- Earnest money is a deposit buyers provide to show they are serious about purchasing a home. It is typically 1% to 5% of the purchase price, though it can sometimes be higher depending on the market, and it is negotiable. While not technically mandatory, most sellers expect it as a sign of commitment and may not take your offer seriously without it.

- The funds are held in escrow and applied toward your closing costs or down payment at the end of the transaction. If the deal falls through for reasons specified in the contract—such as a failed inspection or financing issues—the money is often refundable. However, if you fail to meet your obligations, such as making an unapproved major purchase that disqualifies your loan or backing out without a valid contractual reason, the seller will likely keep the earnest money.

CMA: Your Secret Weapon for a Smart Offer

A **Comparative Market Analysis (CMA)** is a detailed report your real estate agent provides that analyzes the local market. It is like the research basis for pricing your offer.

What is in a CMA?

- **Recent sales** of similar homes in the area (usually within the last 6 months).

- **Listing price vs. sale price**: How close were they? This helps you understand if homes sell above, at, or below the asking price.

- **Comparable Homes:** Many factors influence a home's value. Key considerations include square footage (typically within 200 square feet of the house you are considering), location (distance from subject property), same school district, lot size, number of bathrooms, and other essential features.

- **Days on the market**: The longer a home sits on the market, typically the more negotiating power you might have.

Your agent will use this information to help you craft a competitive yet fair offer. While it might be tempting to start low and negotiate up, be cautious - a lowball offer could backfire by offending the seller or causing you to lose the house to another buyer, especially in a competitive market.

Negotiating: Getting the Best Deal
Without Losing the House

Negotiating can feel like a tango dance. It is all about making the right moves at the right time.

Strategy for Successful Negotiating

- **Know your limits**: Set clear boundaries. Determine the maximum amount you can offer before entering negotiations and commit to it. However, if the home truly feels like your dream home, consider being flexible—do not let a few thousand dollars stand between you and the home you have been searching for.

- **Be flexible**: If the seller does not budge on price, consider asking for concessions such as covering closing costs, helping to buy down your interest rate, and paying for a home warranty, including any appliances, furniture, shed, or lawn equipment that comes with the sale of the house.

- **Stay calm**: It is easy to get emotionally attached, but taking a deep breath, going for a long walk, and keeping a cool head will help you negotiate better.

- **What is important to the seller:** Negotiating is not just about the price; understanding the seller's priorities can give you a real advantage. Some sellers might prioritize a quicker closing timeline, fewer contingencies, or even selling the home as-is to avoid making repairs. Flexibility on the move-out date can also be crucial, especially if the seller needs extra time to transition. By crafting an offer that aligns with these priorities, you can make it more appealing—even if your bid is not the highest.

Here is the reality: in a competitive market, you may have to offer the asking price (or even above it) to win. But in a slower market, you might have room to negotiate down. Your agent's expertise will be key here—trust their advice.

The Role of the Appraiser: Confirming the Value

Even after you agree on a price with the seller, the bank will want to ensure the home is worth that amount. Enter the **appraiser**.

What Does an Appraiser Do?

- They assess the home's value based on its condition, location, and recent comparable sales.
- They provide an **appraisal report** that gives an unbiased estimate of the home's value.

If the appraisal comes in **lower than your offer**, you may have to renegotiate with the seller, or you will often need to bring more cash to the table. If it comes in **at or above the offer**, you are in good shape and can confidently move forward.

Who Pays for What? Breaking Down the Costs

When buying a home, it is essential to understand who covers what during the transaction, as this can play a role in negotiations. For example, if minimizing your out-of-pocket expenses is a priority, you might ask the seller to cover closing costs—but be prepared to offer full price or more. On the other hand, if securing the lowest price is your primary goal, avoid requesting a long list of extras. The key is to prioritize what matters most to you and structure your offer accordingly.

Buyer's Typical Expenses

- **Down payment**: A percentage of the purchase price, usually between 3% and 20%, depending on your loan type. Your lender may have a minimum down payment requirement based on the type of loan, or you may prefer to put more money down.

- **Closing costs**: These can include lender fees, appraisal fees, home inspection fees, title insurance, HOA fees, prepaids (taxes and insurance), and more. Typically, these costs range from 2% to 5% of the purchase price.

- **Home inspection**: Highly recommended! The buyer usually pays this and can reveal any potential issues with the home.

- **Homeowner's insurance**: Required before closing. This protects your investment.

- **HOA transfer fees:** Typically, HOA transfer fees (fees charged by the homeowners association to transfer ownership of the property to the new buyer) are **negotiable** between the buyer and the seller. However, who pays them often depends on local customs, the terms of the purchase contract, and negotiations during the transaction.

  - **In some areas,** Sellers traditionally cover HOA transfer fees as part of closing costs.

  - **In other areas,** Buyers may be expected to pay, especially if the market favors sellers.

  - Always review the purchase agreement carefully and discuss these details with your real estate agent to understand what is customary in your area and how to negotiate if needed.

Seller's Typical Expenses

- **Real estate agent commissions**: Typically around 5% to 7% of the home's sale price, split between the buyer's and seller's agents. (We will dive deeper into commissions later in the book, but for now, remember that they are negotiable, including who pays the real estate agent's commissions. However, opting for a lower commission might mean sacrificing the level of expertise and guidance you need.)

- **Repairs or concessions**: If issues are found during the inspection, the seller may cover the cost of repairs or offer a credit at closing. (Again, this is negotiable, and the seller is NOT required to make the repairs)

- **Prorated property taxes**: Sellers typically pay a prorated amount of property taxes up to the date of closing.

However, these costs are not set in stone. During negotiations, you can ask the seller to cover some of the closing costs or ask for other things, which can help reduce your out-of-pocket expenses.

Warranties: Protecting Your Investment

A **home warranty** is like an insurance policy for your home's major systems and appliances. It is not mandatory, but it is worth considering. If you are **only considering new homes, as long as your builder includes the warranties, you can skip this section on warranties**. However, if you are looking at pre-owned homes, you may want to consider purchasing a home warranty. Sometimes, you can even negotiate for the seller to cover the cost.

What Does a Home Warranty Cover?

- **Appliances**: Think refrigerator, oven, dishwasher, and sometimes the washer and dryer.

- **Systems**: HVAC, plumbing, electrical, and more.

- **Limited repairs**: If something breaks, the warranty may cover the cost of fixing or replacing it, though you may need to pay a deductible or co-pay.

- **Foundation:** Typically included in a builder warranty but probably not on a pre-owned home.

Some sellers include a home warranty as part of the deal to sweeten the offer, while others may agree to pay for one if you ask during negotiations. There are many warranty companies, so be sure to review the specific terms and coverage offered by the company you select.

Final Strategy for Making an Offer

1. **Start with fair market value**: Use the CMA to guide your offer.

2. **Factor in your budget**: When determining your offer, consider your down payment, closing costs, and potential repair costs.

3. **Be strategic**: In a bidding war, your agent may recommend including an **escalation clause**, which automatically increases your offer to a certain amount if someone else bids higher.

4. **Understand contingencies**: Common contingencies include financing, appraisal, and home inspection. These give you legal outs if something goes wrong.

5. **Use the "1-10 scale"**: If you are torn between multiple homes, rate each one on a scale of 1 to 10, considering factors like price, location, condition, and potential. Let this help guide your final decision.

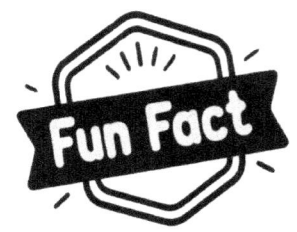

Fun Fact: Did you know that homes typically sell for an average of 98% of their asking price, with many selling for even more in competitive markets? This highlights the importance of realistic pricing and strategic negotiation to gain an edge.

Chapter 4 Key Takeaways

- Understand Fair Market Value: Use factors like location, condition, and comparable sales (comps) to determine a competitive offer.
- Review Seller's Disclosure: Check for any potential issues or repairs to inform your offer.
- Earnest Money Matters: A deposit of 1%-5% of the purchase price shows you are serious and strengthens your offer.
- Negotiate Strategically: Balance price and seller concessions to align with your priorities.
- Include Contingencies: Protect yourself with inspection, financing, and appraisal contingencies.

Summary: Making an offer on a home is a pivotal step in the home-buying process. It requires a mix of careful research, strategic planning, and thoughtful negotiation. From determining the home's fair market value using tools like CMAs to understanding the importance of seller disclosures and earnest money, this chapter walks you through the essentials of crafting a compelling yet realistic offer. Whether negotiating the price or securing concessions, having a clear plan and working closely with your agent can help you confidently navigate this step toward homeownership.

Understanding the market is key to making a competitive yet smart offer. In the next chapter, we will explore how the real estate market influences your home-buying journey.

"FIRST LESSON IN REAL ESTATE: OWN YOUR FIRST PROPERTY."

- BARBARA CORCORAN

Home Sweet Home

Chapter 5

Understanding the Real Estate Market

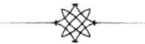

Buying a home is a lot like joining a game where the rules can change at any moment. Various factors influence the real estate market, making prices rise or fall. Understanding these factors can help you make a more intelligent buying decision, time your purchase better, and even save money in the long run.

Why Do Home Prices Go Up and Down?

Home prices do not move randomly. They are influenced by several factors that shift overtime. Here is a quick rundown of just some of what causes prices to go up or down:

Key Factors Influencing Prices

- **Interest rates**: When rates are low, more people think they can afford to buy homes, increasing demand (It is important to note that when rates are low, home prices typically rise).

- **Economic conditions**: A strong economy generally means rising home prices, while a weak economy can lead to a price drop.

- **Government policies**: Tax incentives, interest rate changes, or new housing regulations can all impact home prices.

- **Job Market and Employment Trends:** Areas with growing job opportunities attract more buyers, driving prices up. Conversely, declining job markets can reduce demand and lower prices.

- **Inflation:** Rising inflation increases the cost of building materials and labor, which can lead to higher home prices. It also affects buyers' purchasing power.

- **Population Growth or Decline:** An influx of people to a region increases demand for housing, raising prices. Population decline has the opposite effect, reducing demand and prices.

- **Local Market Conditions:** Neighborhood-specific factors, such as school quality, crime rates, or nearby amenities, can drive prices up or down regardless of national trends.

- **Mortgage Availability:** When lenders tighten credit requirements, fewer people qualify for loans, reducing demand and lowering prices. Easier access to credit has the opposite effect.

The big takeaway here is that the market is like a living organism, it is constantly changing and reacting to new factors. This is why you will sometimes see houses flying off the market or, at other times, sitting there for months.

Supply and Demand: The Heart of the Market

At its core, real estate is driven by **supply and demand**.

Supply

- This is how many homes are available for sale. When there is a lot of supply (many homes for sale), buyers have more choices, and prices tend to stabilize or even fall.

- When supply is low (there are fewer homes for sale), buyers compete for the limited options, driving prices up.

Demand

- Demand refers to the number of buyers actively looking for homes. When demand is high, prices tend to rise.

- Factors that drive demand include low interest rates, a strong job market, and population growth.

More simply put, **more demand + less supply = higher prices**, and **more supply + less demand = lower prices**.

Appreciation: Why Home Values Usually Go Up Over Time

Appreciation is one of the most exciting aspects of buying a home. It is the increase in your home's value over time, and it can be influenced by:

- **Location**: Homes in popular areas (good schools, proximity to jobs, etc.) or have a unique appeal like lake life, close to entertainment, or anything with a significant appeal will often appreciate faster.

- **Improvements**: Renovating a kitchen, adding a bathroom, or even adding a shower to a ½ bath can boost a home's value.

- **Market trends**: A strong economy or growing demand can cause values to rise across the board.

However, appreciation is not always guaranteed. In some cases, home values can decrease, especially during economic downturns. However, over the long term, real estate has generally been a sound investment that tends to appreciate.

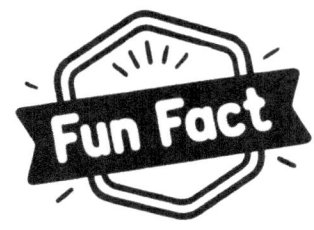

Fun Fact: Homes in the U.S. typically appreciate at an average annual rate of **3% to 5%**, and in rapidly growing times or areas, this rate can be higher, even 10-15% or more. While the Federal Reserve targets a **2% inflation rate**, the long-term average inflation rate in the U.S. is around **3.2%.** This means that, in most cases, your home's value grows faster than inflation, offering you a powerful hedge against rising costs and building equity over time.

Buyer's Market vs. Seller's Market: Timing Matters

When you hear people talking about a **buyer's market** or a **seller's market**, they are referring to who has the upper hand in negotiations.

In real estate, **inventory** refers to the number of homes available for sale. The amount of inventory is measured in terms of how many months it would take to sell all the available homes at the current sales pace, assuming no new listings come on the market.

6 months of inventory is typically considered a **balanced or level market**, where supply and demand are relatively equal. In this scenario, neither buyers nor sellers have a significant advantage. Prices generally remain stable.

Buyer's Market

- **What is it?** It occurs when there are more homes for sale than buyers looking to purchase.

- **How does it affect you?** You have more leverage to negotiate a lower price, request repairs, or get the seller to cover some closing costs.

- **Signs of a buyer's market**: Homes are staying on the market longer, sellers are offering incentives, and prices may drop.

- **More than 6 months of inventory** is considered a **buyer's market** because supply exceeds demand. Sellers may need to lower prices or offer incentives to attract buyers, giving buyers the upper hand.

Seller's Market

- **What is it?** This is when there are more buyers than there are homes for sale.

- **How does it affect you?** Be prepared for bidding wars, higher prices, and fewer seller concessions.

- **Signs of a seller's market**: Homes sell quickly, often with multiple offers, and prices tend to rise.

- **Less than 6 months of inventory** is considered a **seller's market** because demand outpaces supply. With fewer homes available, buyers compete for limited properties, often driving up prices.

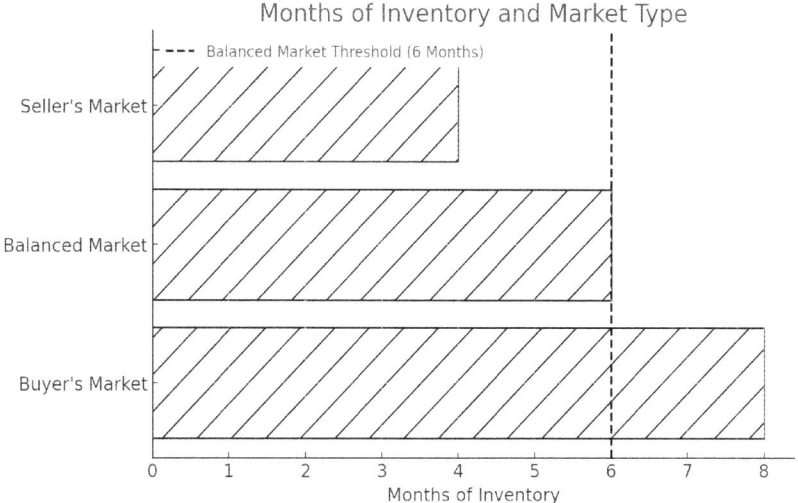

Months of Inventory and Market Type

Example 1: Seller's Market

- **Scenario:** A desirable urban area experiences a boom in job opportunities, attracting a large influx of people. The housing inventory drops to 3 months because homes sell quickly, and new listings cannot keep up with demand.

- **Result:** Buyers face bidding wars and may need to offer above the asking price to secure a home.

Example 2: Buyer's Market

- **Scenario:** A suburban area sees a decline in demand due to a major employer relocating. Housing inventory increases to 9 months because fewer people buy, and homes stay on the market longer.

- **Result:** Buyers can negotiate lower prices, request repairs, or ask sellers to cover closing costs since sellers are eager to make a deal.

This concept is a key indicator for assessing the health of a housing market and helps buyers and sellers set realistic expectations. Knowing whether it is a buyer's or seller's market can help you strategize your offer, negotiate better, and understand what to expect.

The Cost of Not Buying a Home

You might think, "What if I wait for the market to cool down?" While that is a fair question, there is also a **cost to not buying a home**—and it is worth understanding.

Financial Costs

- **Renting is 100% interest**: When you rent, you pay your landlord's mortgage instead of building your own equity.

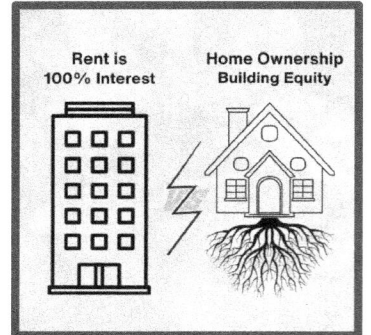

- **Missing out on appreciation**: Waiting can mean paying more for the same property later as home values rise.

- **Inflation**: The cost of living typically increases over time, as do home prices. This means a home that is budget-friendly now might not be affordable in a few years.

Lifestyle Costs

- **Lack of stability**: Renting means you could face rent increases or be forced to move if your landlord decides to sell.

- **Limited freedom**: You cannot always customize your living space or make changes to suit your preferences.

This does not mean you should rush into buying a home. It just means there is a cost to waiting, and you should factor that into your decision-making process.

Final Tips for Navigating the Market

1. **Stay informed**: Monitor market trends, interest rates, and local developments that could affect home prices.

2. **Be ready to act**: Have your finances in order, be pre-approved for a mortgage, and work closely with your agent to stay ahead of the competition.

3. **Be patient but prepared**: Finding the right home takes time, regardless of whether the market is buyer's or seller's market. Do not hesitate to hold out for the right home but avoid overanalyzing or waiting too long. When the right opportunity comes along, be ready to act swiftly.

Top Points to Remember

Understanding the real estate market can feel like trying to predict the weather. It is complex, influenced by many factors, and not always easy to forecast. But with a good grasp of supply and demand, appreciation, market types, and the cost of waiting, you will be better equipped to make intelligent decisions.

Remember, the market will always fluctuate, but your focus should be on finding a home that fits your needs and budget. If you buy a home that you love, in a place where you want to live, at a price you can afford, you have won—regardless of the market conditions.

And when you finally close on your new home, you will have a front-row seat to watch it (hopefully) appreciate over time. Maybe you will even have a dinner out with friends or a dance-it-out party. Why not? You have earned it.

Decoding Your Local Real Estate Market: A Beginner's Guide and Why Local Market Knowledge Matters

When Gabriel and Sarah decided to buy their first home, they assumed that real estate markets were uniform across the country. They quickly learned that this was not the case. Their friend, Lisa, had recently purchased a home in a small town in the Midwest, where properties were affordable, and bidding wars were rare. In contrast, Gabriel and Sarah were house hunting in a bustling coastal city, where homes sold above the asking price within days.

The Importance of Local Market Knowledge

Understanding that real estate markets vary significantly by region, Gabriel and Sarah realized they needed to educate themselves about their local market. They discovered that factors such as job growth, population trends, and local amenities heavily influence property values and market dynamics.

Diving into Local Data

To gain insights into their area's market, they turned to several resources:

Here is the revised version of your list with both clickable links for digital readers and full URLs for print readers:

Best Real Estate Market Research Sites

- **Zillow Research:** This platform offers data on home values, market trends, and forecasts specific to various regions.
  - Website: https://www.zillow.com/research

- **Realtor.com Research:** Provides comprehensive housing data and real estate market trends, including weekly and monthly updates.
  - Website: https://www.realtor.com/research
- **Redfin Data Center:** Offers downloadable housing market data, including information on home prices, sales, and inventory levels.
  - Website: https://www.redfin.com/news/data-center
- **National Association of REALTORS® (NAR):** Publishes housing statistics and real estate market trends on national, regional, and metro-market levels.
  - Website: https://www.nar.realtor/research-and-statistics
- **Texas REALTORS® Market Research:** A particularly useful resource for state-specific market data, especially for buyers in Texas.
  - Website:https://www.texasrealestate.com/market-research

Analyzing the Data

By exploring these resources, Gabriel and Sarah learned that their city's real estate market was highly competitive, with limited inventory and rising prices. They discovered that homes in their desired neighborhood sold within days, often above the listing price. This information helped them set realistic expectations and develop a strategic approach.

Cut Through the Noise: Let an Expert Guide You

Feeling overwhelmed by all the market research, trends, and navigating a buyer's or seller's market? Simplify the process by hiring an experienced real estate agent who knows the market inside out and can make your home-buying journey smoother.

Key Insights from the Experts

**Seth & Jocelyn Mills,
Real Estate Agents**

What great agents do when working with buyers:

1. **Find the right home:** Great real estate agents have access to large networks of people and homes, creating off-market and pre-market opportunities. They can search more broadly and completely for all available listings through trade organizations, state agencies, and brokerage technologies. These professional resources, coupled with extensive search experience, make it possible to eliminate distractions and hone in on the few homes that best suit buyers' personalized needs.

2. **Negotiate terms:** Home-buying can be an emotional rollercoaster, and agents help to keep clear objectives and cooler heads. They also provide critical insight into market norms, tactical advantages, and proven strategic models.

3. **Understand the home-buying process:** Complicated contracts, extensive financing options, and ever-changing transactional rules are an agent's job to help navigate. Buyers gain access to needed documents and verified service providers to maximize purchasing power and minimize surprise setbacks.

What great buyers do when working with agents:

1. **Interview and select your Real Estate agent early. Ask questions!** Great buyers gain access to professional resources as early as possible, as credit repair and new construction can be 12-month processes! They also seek agents that match their communication style and service expectations.

2. **Share the big picture and the small details:** Casting a vision and crafting the plan for a home purchase is a collaborative effort between a buyer and their agent. They must be open and honest about changes of heart and obstacles of all kinds (timing, finances, desire, etc.).

3. **Embrace the process and stay informed:** Every home purchase follows a plan, with contingencies designed for when things go sideways. Successful buyers stay proactive—researching neighborhoods, providing documents to lenders promptly, and making timely decisions. They expect regular updates, usually weekly, unless changes in the transaction require more immediate communication.

Seth & Jocelyn Mills
Texas Sold Em Realty Group

Common Mistakes to Avoid

1. **Assuming All Markets Are the Same**: Believing that real estate trends are uniform can lead to misguided decisions. Always research your specific area's market conditions.

2. **Ignoring Local Economic Indicators**: Factors like employment rates, local business growth, and infrastructure developments can significantly impact property values.

3. **Overlooking Seasonal Trends**: Real estate activity can vary with seasons. For instance, spring often sees more listings and higher competition. Many families like to move and get settled before school starts up again.

Chapter 5 Key Takeaways

- **Do Your Homework**: Utilize online resources to gather data on your local real estate market.

- **Consult Local Experts**: Engage with local real estate agents with firsthand knowledge of the area's market dynamics.

- **Stay Informed**: Real estate markets are constantly evolving. Regularly update your knowledge to make informed decisions.

By immersing themselves in local market data and consulting with knowledgeable professionals, Gabriel and Sarah could confidently navigate their home-buying journey. They understood the importance of tailoring their approach to their specific market, ultimately finding a home that met their needs and budget. Remember, knowledge isn't just power in real estate, it is peace of mind.

Chapter 6

Finance 101:
Mastering the Mortgage Maze

Understanding home financing is crucial to navigating the path to homeownership. It is not the most glamorous part of buying a home, but it is one of the most important. Let's break down the essentials so you can approach your mortgage with confidence and avoid feeling lost in the process.

What is a Mortgage?

Unless you are paying cash, A mortgage is a loan that helps you buy a home. The lender provides the funds, which you repay with interest over a set term, typically 15 to 30 years. The most common choice is a 30-year fixed-rate mortgage.

Key Components of a Mortgage:

- **PITI** Stands for principal, interest, taxes, and insurance
    - **Principal:** The amount borrowed.
    - **Interest:** The cost of borrowing money.
    - **Taxes:** Refers to your property taxes
    - **Insurance:** Insurance for your home
- **Term:** The length of time to repay the loan.
- **HOA Fees:** Homeowners Association - If applicable, these may not be included in your monthly mortgage payment and must be factored into your budget.

Example of PITI (Principle, interest, taxes, and insurance) With 5% Down Payment

Home Price	Interest Rate	Principal & Interest	Taxes	Insurance	Total Payment
$200,000	6%	$1,139.15	$208.33	$58.33	$1,405.81
$200,000	8%	$1,394.15	$208.33	$58.33	$1,660.82
$200,000	10%	$1,667.39	$208.33	$58.33	$1,934.05
$400,000	6%	$2,278.29	$416.67	$116.67	$2,811.63
$400,000	8%	$2,788.31	$416.67	$116.67	$3,321.64
$400,000	10%	$3,334.77	$416.67	$116.67	$3,868.11
$600,000	6%	$3,417.44	$625.00	$175.00	$4,217.44
$600,000	8%	$4,182.46	$625.00	$175.00	$4,982.46
$600,000	10%	$5,002.16	$625.00	$175.00	$5,802.16

This example highlights the importance of asking your lender the right questions. Many first-time buyers are confused by online mortgage calculators that show only Principal and Interest (PI), excluding Taxes and Insurance, which are essential parts of the total monthly cost. Understanding the full PITI (Principal, Interest, Taxes, and Insurance) is crucial for accurate budgeting. Taxes and insurance rates can vary significantly. Property taxes states like New Jersey, Illinois, and Texas, property taxes may be double or more compared to rural areas. That is why getting an accurate payment estimate tailored to your location from your lender is vital.

Amortization Demystified:
Why You Pay More Interest Upfront

Mortgage payments are structured using a process called amortization. With a 30-year fixed-rate mortgage, the most common loan type, the lender divides the loan into equal monthly payments for principal and interest (PI) over the loan term. However, there are other types of loans available, such as 15-year fixed-rate, adjustable-rate mortgages (ARMs), and programs can vary depending on your needs and qualifications. In the early years of a fixed-rate mortgage, a larger portion of each payment goes toward interest, while only a small amount reduces the principal balance. This happens because interest is calculated on the remaining loan balance, which is highest at the beginning. Over time, as the principal decreases, the interest portion of each payment shrinks, and more is applied directly to the principal. Understanding this gradual shift is crucial for recognizing the long-term impact of early payments and interest costs. Remember, your property taxes and insurance can vary and may affect your overall payment, referred to as principal, interest, taxes, and insurance (PITI).

Description: This chart illustrates the breakdown of mortgage payments for a $450,000 home with a 30-year fixed loan at an 8% annual interest rate. It highlights how much of the monthly payment is allocated toward the principal versus the interest at specific points during the loan term: Year 1 and every 5 years thereafter.

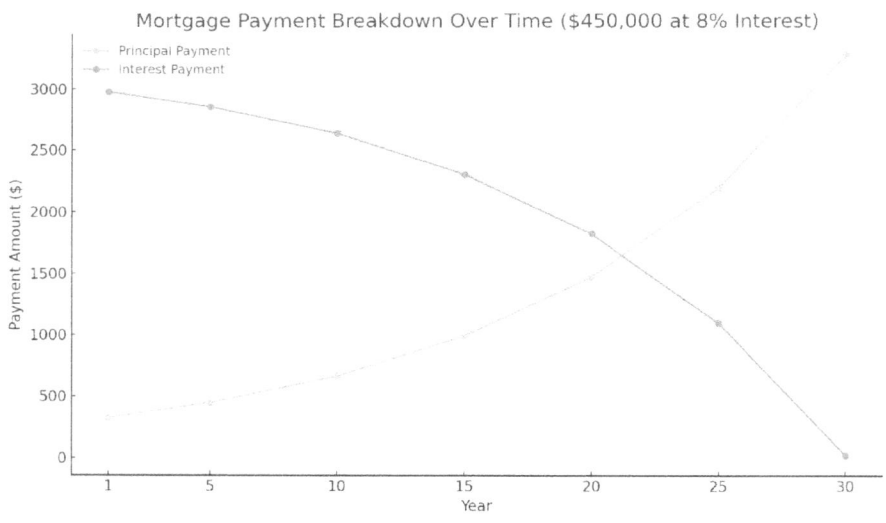

Year	Principal Payment	Interest Payment	Remaining Balance
1	$ 302	$ 3,000	$ 449,698
5	$ 447	$ 2,855	$ 427,814
10	$ 666	$ 2,636	$ 394,761
15	$ 992	$ 2,310	$ 345,517
20	$ 1,478	$ 1,824	$ 272,151
25	$ 2,202	$ 1,100	$ 162,847
30	$ 3,280	$ 22	$ -

Disclaimer: This is a approximate simplified example based on standard amortization. Actual payments may vary due to taxes, insurance, or lender-specific terms. Consult a financial advisor or mortgage professional for personalized advice.

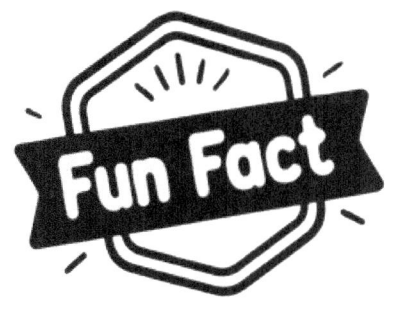

Fun Fact: The Magic of Extra Payments: By paying an additional $275 per month (equivalent to one extra payment per year), less than the cost of 1 or 2 fancy daily lattes— you can say goodbye to **7 years** of mortgage payments and own your home in **23 years instead of 30**!

How Lenders Qualify You

Lenders assess your financial situation to determine your borrowing capacity. Key factors include:

- **Credit Score:** Higher scores lead to better rates and terms.
- **Income:** Verifies your ability to make monthly payments.
- **Debt-to-Income Ratio (DTI):** The percentage of your income used for debt payments.

Key Ratios:

1. **Front-End Ratio:** Housing costs should generally not exceed 28-31% of your gross income.
2. **Back-End Ratio:** Total debt payments, including the mortgage (PITI) and HOA, should typically not exceed 43-50% of gross income.

For example, if your household income is $200,000 annually, your maximum front-end ratio would cap your housing costs at $5,000 per month, while your total debt payments, including the mortgage, would be capped at $8,333 per month. Refer to your gross income level below to determine your maximum front-end and back-end ratios. *(Gross income is your total income before any taxes or deductions are taken out of your paycheck.)*

Yearly Income	Front Ratio Monthly Mortgage Payment %	Back Ratio DTI ALL Debt to Income %
	30%	50%
$80,500	$2,013	$3,354
$100,000	$2,500	$4,167
$120,000	$3,000	$5,000
$140,000	$3,500	$5,833
$160,000	$4,000	$6,667
$180,000	$4,500	$7,500
$200,000	$5,000	$8,333
$220,000	$5,500	$9,167
$240,000	$6,000	$10,000
$260,000	$6,500	$10,833
$280,000	$7,000	$11,667
$300,000	$7,500	$12,500
$400,000	$10,000	$16,667
$500,000	$12,500	$20,833

*This is for example purposes only. For more detailed information on the right loan/plan for you please check with your lender as programs and terms vary.

Buydowns: Lowering Your Interest Rate

A buydown allows you to reduce your interest rate:

- **Temporary Buydown:** Lowers the rate for a set period, reducing initial payments.

- **Permanent Buydown:** Lowers the rate for the life of the loan.

Buydowns can be a good strategy if you want lower payments early on or plan to refinance later.

Prequalification: Know Your Buying Power

Before shopping for homes, **get prequalified FIRST** by a professional mortgage lender. This gives you a clear picture of your budget and helps you focus on homes you can afford. It is important to note that being prequalified and preapproved are not the same - more details on pre-approval are coming up.

Benefits of Prequalification:

- **Sets a realistic budget:** Avoid falling in love with homes outside your price range.

- **Strengthens your offer:** Sellers take prequalified buyers more seriously.

- **Builds financial confidence:** Understand your affordability range and monthly payment comfort zone.

Down Payments: How Much Do You Need?

The down payment is a significant part of your upfront costs.

Choosing the Right Mortgage: Loan Types Simplified

- **FHA Loans:** The Federal Housing Administration requires a minimum of 3.5%. Great for first-time buyers with lower credit scores or limited savings.
  - A credit score of 580 or higher, or some lenders will go as low as 500 and 579, but this may require a higher down payment of at least 10%.

- FHA loan limits, the maximum amounts FHA will insure, vary by area and local housing costs. Use HUD's online tool at https://entp.hud.gov/idapp/html/hicostlook.cfm to search limits by state and county for single-family and multi-family homes.

- **Conventional Loans:** Typically require 5-20%, though some programs allow as little as 3% for qualified buyers. It is best for buyers with strong credit and larger down payments.
  - The typical minimum credit score for a conventional loan is 620

- **Jumbo Loans:** A jumbo loan exceeds the conventional loan limit for the area, typically loans over $800,000.
  - The typical minimum credit score for a conventional loan is 620. A higher credit score often leads to better interest rates and terms.

- **VA Loans:** Often require no down payment for qualified veterans.
  - The VA does not set a minimum credit score, but most lenders require 580-620.

- **USDA Loans:** 100% financing for homes in eligible rural or suburban areas.
  - USDA does not mandate a credit score, but lenders typically prefer **640+** for easier approval.

Many other loan programs exist, but these account for roughly 90% of home loans. While general guidelines provide a baseline, each lender sets its own requirements, ranging from more flexible to stricter standards. To find the best fit, it is wise to consult multiple lenders and compare their criteria. The mortgage process can feel overwhelming, but your carefully chosen lender is there to guide you every step of the way.

Can I Put More Down? Yes, but consider whether those funds could be better used elsewhere, such as paying off high-interest debt or building an emergency fund. Consider that a larger down payment can lower monthly payments not only by putting more down but also by eliminating private mortgage insurance (PMI).

Sources for Down Payment Funds:

- Personal savings
- Gifts from family
- 401(k) loans or withdrawals
- Down payment assistance programs
- Employer Programs (rare but worth checking on)
- Tax Refunds
- Equity from other property
- Sell some valuables or investments
- Life insurance policy that has a cash value
- Bitcoin or cryptocurrency
- Special loan programs: Some loan types, like VA or USDA loans, do not require a down payment, freeing up your savings for other expenses.

Reserves: Your Safety Net Lenders may require you to have **reserves**, which are extra savings that cover a few months' worth of mortgage payments. This provides a financial cushion and improves your approval odds.

Why Reserves Matter:

- **Stability:** Helps cover unexpected expenses.

- **Approval Chances:** Demonstrates financial security to lenders.

Understanding Your Mortgage: Key Components and Terms

ARM vs. Fixed-Rate Loans:

- **Fixed-rate mortgage**: The interest rate remains the same throughout the loan term.

- **Adjustable-rate mortgage (ARM)**: Rate changes after an initial period could mean lower initial payments but potential increases later.

Mortgage Points: How They Work

What Are Mortgage Points? Mortgage points, or discount points, are optional upfront fees paid at closing to lower your loan's interest rate. Each point costs 1% of the loan amount and typically reduces the rate by 0.25%.

Example:

- Loan: $200,000 at 6% interest.
- Buying 2 points costs $4,000 (2% of $200,000) and reduces the rate to 5.5%.
- Monthly Savings: $63 ($1,199 at 6% vs. $1,136 at 5.5%).
- Break-Even Point: 64 months (just over 5 years).

Key Considerations:

- It is best for buyers who plan to stay in the home long-term.
- Selling or refinancing early may not recover the cost.
- Always ask your lender if points fit your financial goals.

Points can reduce long-term costs if used strategically.

Mortgage Insurance: PMI vs. MIP

If your down payment is less than 20%, you will likely need mortgage insurance:

- **PMI (Private Mortgage Insurance):** Required for conventional loans. It can often be canceled once you reach 20% equity.

- **MIP (Mortgage Insurance Premium):** Required for FHA loans. Includes an upfront premium and monthly payments. It may last for the life of the loan.

Loan-to-Value (LTV) Ratio: Why It Matters

LTV compares your loan amount to the property's value and influences loan approval, interest rates, and the need for mortgage insurance. Lower LTV means more equity and less lender risk.

Example: If you are purchasing a $200,000 home and borrowing $180,000, your LTV is 90%. Lenders may require PMI for LTVs above 80%.

Escrow Accounts: Managing Taxes and Insurance

An escrow account, managed by your lender, holds funds for property taxes and homeowners insurance, ensuring these bills are paid on time. This avoids large lump-sum payments and simplifies budgeting. Many lenders require escrow accounts for borrowers with down payments under 20%.

Down Payment Assistance Programs Many programs help with down payments, especially for first-time buyers, but availability varies by area and is not always available. Consult local mortgage companies and your real estate agent to explore your options.

Types of Assistance:

- **State or Local Programs:** Grants, loans, or tax credits.

- **Employer-Assisted Housing:** Some employers offer home-buying aid.

- **Nonprofits:** Provide grants or zero-interest loans.

When Will My House Payments Start?
Your first mortgage payment is typically due one month after the last day of the closing month. For example, if you close in April, your first payment is due on June 1st.

Interest-Rate Strategy: "Marry the House, Date the Rate"

This popular phrase reminds buyers to focus on finding the right home now, even if interest rates are not perfect.

- **Marry the house**: Commit to the right home for your needs and budget.

- **Date the rate**: If rates drop in the future, you can refinance for a lower payment.

Why This Strategy Works

- **Home values tend to rise**: Waiting for lower rates could mean paying more for the same home.

- **Refinancing options**: If rates fall, you can "break up" with the old rate.

FHA or Conventional?
Finding the Loan That Fits Your Needs

Understanding the differences between FHA and conventional loans is essential when choosing a home loan. Let's examine how Emily and Jake, two first-time homebuyers, navigated their options.

Emily's FHA Loan Journey

Emily, a recent college graduate, had a credit score of 600 and limited savings. She wanted to purchase a modest home but was unsure about qualifying for a loan. After consulting a mortgage advisor, she learned about FHA loans, insured by the Federal Housing Administration, which are ideal for borrowers with lower credit scores and smaller down payments.

- **Credit Score:** Emily's 600 score qualified her for an FHA loan, which requires a minimum score of 580 for a 3.5% down payment.

- **Down Payment:** She put down $7,000 on a $200,000 home.

- **Mortgage Insurance:** FHA loans require an upfront mortgage insurance premium (UFMIP) and an annual mortgage insurance premium (MIP), which were included in Emily's closing costs and monthly payments.

- **Loan Limits:** Emily ensured her home price was within the FHA loan limit for her area.

Jake's Conventional Loan Path

Jake, a young professional, had a 720 credit score and substantial savings. He aimed to buy a suburban home and chose a conventional loan.

- **Credit Score:** Jake's 720 score qualified him for competitive terms, as conventional loans usually require a minimum score of 620.

- **Down Payment:** He opted for 20%, or $80,000, on a $400,000 home, eliminating the need for private mortgage insurance (PMI).

- **Loan Limits:** Conventional loans often have higher limits, giving Jake more options in high-cost areas.

Essential Insights:

- **Credit Flexibility:** FHA loans are better for lower credit scores, while conventional loans reward higher scores with better terms.

- **Down Payment:** FHA loans require as little as 3.5%, while conventional loans may need more but allow you to avoid PMI with 20%.

- **Mortgage Insurance:** FHA loans always include mortgage insurance, while conventional loans can waive it with sufficient equity.

Emily and Jake's stories show how personal finances influence loan choices. Working with a mortgage professional can help you weigh your options and choose the best loan for your needs.

Secret for Finding the Right Lender

The right lender can make a huge difference in your home-buying experience.

Tips for Finding the Right Lender:

- **Compare Multiple Lenders:** Shop around for the best mix of rates, terms, fees, and a lender you feel comfortable working with. The lowest rate means little if the lender cannot close on time. A slightly higher rate with excellent customer service may save you stress and costly mistakes.

- **Read Reviews:** Check feedback from other buyers.

- **Ask Questions:** Understand their process, communication style, and fees. TIP: Request a written fee list.

- **Seek Referrals:** Trusted recommendations from friends, family, or your real estate agent (typically your BEST referral source) often lead to lenders known for excellent service and smooth transactions.

- **Home Builders:** Builders often have in-house lenders with incentives. While you can choose any lender, compare builder's loan terms with others to ensure they meet your needs. Keep in mind that the builder's incentives can be pretty compelling and may make their lender the best option for your situation.

- **Do not Give Up:** Finding the right lender might require speaking with 3-10 lenders or more. Each lender offers different programs, so do not take "no" as an absolute answer. Keep searching for the lender and loan program that fits your specific needs, it is worth the effort!

Key Insights From The Experts

**Alfonso Guzman,
Mortgage Loan Officer**

1. What types of mortgage loans do you offer, and which would be best for my situation?

2. How much can I potentially borrow based on my income and debt-to-income ratio?

3. What are the down payment requirements for different loan programs?

4. What credit score do I need to qualify for various loan options?

5. Do you offer pre-approval, and what does that process involve?

6. What fees and monthly payments can I expect with different loan options?

7. Are there any down payment assistance programs I might qualify for?

8. How will you keep me updated throughout the loan process?

9. What documentation will I need to provide for the loan application?

10. How long does the loan approval process typically take?

By asking these questions, you can gain valuable insights into the loan officer's expertise, communication style, and ability to meet your specific needs as a homebuyer.

The most important thing to do while in the process of loan approval is PLEASE ALWAYS MAKE SURE YOU DISCUSS ANY FINANCIAL SPENDING WITH YOUR LOAN OFFICER, ESPECIALLY WHEN IT COMES DOWN TO MOVING MONEY AROUND OR APPLYING FOR NEW DEBT. Never do any moves like that unless you have the green light from your trusted loan officer.

Alfonso Guzman Sr Loan Officer, NMLS 1191940
Ignite Loan Partners | Mortgage Broker

"I ALWAYS FELT VERY SECURE AND VERY SAFE WITH REAL ESTATE. REAL ESTATE ALWAYS APPRECIATES."

- IVANA TRUMP

Home Sweet Home

Checklist of Documents Most Lenders Will Require

To make the process smoother, gather these documents early:

- Recent pay stubs
- W-2s or 1099s from the last 2 years
- Personal Bank statements (last 2-3 months)
- Personal Tax returns (last 2 years)
- Proof of additional income
- ID and Social Security number
- Proof of Down Payment
    - Documentation showing the source of your down payment (e.g., bank statements, gift letters, if applicable)
    - Sale of assets documentation (if funds are coming from sold property or items)
- Other Documents, if applicable:
    - Divorce decrees or separation agreements
    - Bankruptcy discharge papers
    - Explanation for any derogatory credit items
    - Rental history or landlord contact information (for first-time buyers)
    - Documentation of any other financial obligations, like child support or alimony
- Self Employed? You will need all of the above plus likely the list below
    - Minimum 2 years of business tax returns

- ☐ Year-to-date profit and loss (P&L) statement for your business
- ☐ Balance Sheet
- ☐ Business License
- ☐ Business Bank Statements

This is a general checklist to get you started gathering all your information and putting it in one folder for easy access. Each lender may have slightly different requirements, so it is always best to confirm their specific needs beforehand.

Why Does My Lender Keep Asking for More?

It is normal to feel frustrated when lenders request more documents, but it is part of the process. Your application goes through underwriters, processors, and quality control, each with specific requirements. Provide requested items quickly to avoid delays. New requests may arise—this is standard. Stay calm, organized, and focused; every step brings you closer to your dream home!

Buying a Home Without a Social Security Number (SSN)

If you have a Social Security number, you can skip this part.

Yes, you can buy a house in the United States without a SSN, often using an Individual Taxpayer Identification Number (ITIN). This is sometimes needed for various reasons, often tied to their immigration or residency status. The process differs and comes with specific requirements:

1. **ITIN Loans:** Designed for those without a SSN but paying U.S. taxes.
2. Documentation: Proof of identity, income, ITIN, tax returns, and bank statements are required.

3. **Down Payment:** Typically, 15-25%, depending on the lender.
4. **Credit History:** Alternative credit forms, like utility or rent payments, may be accepted.
5. **Loan Availability:** Not all lenders offer ITIN loans; seek specialized lenders or community banks.
6. **Legal Residency:** A visa or legal residency is not required, but it may impact loan options.
7. **Cash Purchases:** No ITIN or SSN is needed if paying cash, but fund sources must be documented.
8. **Limitations:** ITIN loans have higher rates and stricter requirements. Federal programs like FHA, VA, or USDA loans require an SSN.

Work with an experienced agent and lender familiar with ITIN loans to navigate the process.

Fun Fact: On average, homeowners save thousands over renters in the long term, thanks to tax benefits and equity growth!

Chapter 6 Key Takeaways

- **Know Your Mortgage:** Understand all components (PITI) for accurate budgeting.

- **Loan Qualification:** Credit, income, and debt ratios determine approval.

- **Loan Types:** FHA, VA, USDA, and Conventional loans cover most needs.

- **Down Payments:** Save from various sources; larger amounts lower costs.

- **Prequalification:** Clarifies budget and strengthens offers.

- **Find the Right Lender:** Compare options; persistence pays off.
- **Tip:** Focus on finding the right home and refinance rates later.

Summary: Navigating the mortgage process can feel daunting, but with preparation, a clear budget, and a trusted team, you can make informed decisions that lead to your dream of homeownership. It is not just about finding the ideal house—it is about making smart financial choices that ensure long-term stability. With the right approach, you will find a home you love and set yourself up for lasting success. And that is something worth celebrating!

"HOME OWNERSHIP IS THE CORNERSTONE OF A STRONG COMMUNITY."

– RICK RENZI

Home Sweet Home

Share Your Journey, Inspire Others!

Thanks for continuing your journey with *Home Sweet Home*.
If you have found value in this guide, sharing a quick review
could help others take the leap toward homeownership.
Your insights could inspire someone else
to make their dreams a reality.

Making a difference is *easy!*

Just scan the QR code or click the link below
to share your review:

https://a.co/d/62i4TOQ

Your effort to contribute to the conversation and share
good vibes are deeply appreciated—
thank you for making a difference!

Thanks again, Sally Street

Chapter 7:

Top 10 Mortgage Hurdles and How to Overcome Them!

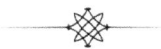

Applying for a mortgage can feel like running an obstacle course, with each hurdle requiring a little more effort than the last. However, knowing what to expect will help you navigate the process with confidence. This chapter highlights the most common challenges buyers face and provides practical solutions to overcome them. Let's dive in and make this journey as smooth as possible!

1. Low Credit Score: A low credit score is one of the most common barriers to getting approved for a mortgage. Lenders see it as a sign of risk, which can result in higher interest rates or outright rejection. In a later chapter, we will explore credit and credit scores in greater depth.

How to Overcome It:

- **Check your credit report** for errors and dispute any inaccuracies.

- **Pay down existing debts** to improve your debt-to-income ratio.

- **Establish good credit habits**, like paying bills on time and keeping credit card balances low.

- **Consider an FHA loan**, which is more lenient and has lower credit score requirements.

- **Boost Your Credit Score with Authorized User Status:** If you have a loved one with excellent credit, ask them to add you as an authorized user on one of their credit cards. This allows you to benefit from their positive payment history and low credit utilization, which can significantly improve your credit score over time. This strategy can help you qualify for better loan terms and mortgage rates if the account is well-managed.

- **Rapid Re-score: Fix It Fast, Score It Faster:** Often used by your mortgage lender or mortgage broker to quickly update your credit scores. Example: If you have paid off a balance or resolved a credit error, a rapid re-score accelerates updates to your credit report and score. Ideal for mortgage applicants or others with tight timelines, it provides a quick way to reflect improvements in your financial profile.

2. High Debt-to-Income Ratio (DTI): Lenders want to ensure that you can manage your debt payments comfortably. A high DTI indicates that you are already carrying a significant amount of debt, making you a higher-risk **borrower.**

How to Overcome It:

When thinking about buying a home, paying attention to your debt-to-income (DTI) ratio is key. Start by listing all your debts, monthly payments, and interest rates to pinpoint where your efforts can make the biggest difference. But do not stop there—getting prequalified is a smarter move. Opt for a soft credit pull to protect your score, and lean on a professional for guidance. They can help you set SMART goals—Specific, Measurable, Achievable, Relevant, and Time-bound—that make your financial improvements focused and attainable, paving the way to homeownership.

- **Example 1:** David had a $600 monthly car payment with only 3 months remaining. He decided to pay off his vehicle first, freeing up that money to tackle other debts.

- **Example 2:** Victoria had a $250 monthly car payment with 4 years left and three credit cards. After reviewing her debts, she noticed one credit card carried an 18% interest rate with a $2,000 balance. Focusing on this high-interest debt, she prioritized paying it off before rolling the extra money into paying down her other cards. To accelerate progress, she transferred the balances on two cards to a 0% interest offer, enabling her to pay everything off within 6 months. Now, Victoria pays off her credit cards monthly and keeps her usage below 10% of the credit limit, which has significantly boosted her credit score.

- **Example 3:** Lisa had multiple high-interest credit cards with a total balance of $10,000 and an average interest rate of 22%. Struggling to make progress on her payments, she visited her local credit union to explore options. The credit union offered her a consolidation loan with a fixed interest rate of 9%, significantly lower than her credit cards. By consolidating her debt, Lisa reduced her monthly payment and simplified her finances, freeing up extra cash to save for her home down payment. Over time, her improved payment history and reduced credit utilization also helped boost her credit score, making her a more attractive borrower for a mortgage.

Which debts to tackle first? Contact a mortgage company early in the process and ask for expert guidance tailored to your situation.

Increase your income by getting a raise, getting a higher-paying job in the same career field, or taking on extra work. There are a lot of side gigs or gig jobs available. Are you qualified? These extra funds will help you pay down debt quicker and improve your ratio.

- **Consider a co-borrower**, such as a parent, grandparent, spouse, or partner, to strengthen your application.

3. Lack of Down Payment Funds: Saving for a down payment can be a significant challenge, especially with rising home prices and the cost of living.

How to Overcome It:

- **Down Payment Assistance Programs:** Check for state or local government programs to help you with your down payment.
- **Low Down Payment Loan Options:** Consider FHA, VA, or some conventional loans that require a smaller down payment.
- **Aggressive Saving:** Cut non-essential expenses and establish a clear savings goal to build your down payment fund.
- **Gift Funds:** Funds gifted from a parent or loved one can be used toward your down payment. The lender usually requires a gift letter from the giver to verify it is not a loan.
- **401(k):** Borrowing from your 401(k) is another common option for accessing down payment funds. Be sure to understand the terms and any potential penalties before proceeding.
- **Rent vs. Own: Flip Your Payment Timing and Build "Secret Savings."** Did you know that when you rent, you are paying for the month ahead, but when you own, your mortgage payment is for the month that just passed? This

timing flip creates a "secret savings" during your first month of homeownership! That extra cushion can be a game-changer, helping you cover moving expenses, buy furniture, or even celebrate your big move with a housewarming party. It is like a hidden perk of becoming a homeowner!

4. Employment Issues: Lenders prefer stable, reliable income and typically require at least two years in the same or a related field. Frequent job changes or employment gaps can be red flags, though college or a degree in the same field may count toward this timeframe.

How to Overcome It:

- **Provide a clear explanation** for any job changes or gaps, emphasizing how it is strengthened your position.

- **Show continuous employment history** in the same field, even if you have changed jobs.

- **Consider waiting** until you have been at your current job for at least 6 months to 1 year before applying.

Always discuss your situation with your lender to see how they interpret employment history in the context of your education. This approach varies depending on the loan type and lender policies.

5. Not Getting Prequalified: Some buyers go house hunting without knowing what they can afford, leading to disappointment or financial strain.

How to Overcome It:

- **Get prequalified** before you start looking at homes. This will help you understand your budget and strengthen your negotiating position.
- **Review the prequalification carefully**, considering your comfort level with the estimated payments.

6. Interest Rate Fluctuations: Interest rates can change rapidly, affecting your loan's affordability and monthly payments.

How to Overcome It:

- **Lock in your interest rate** once you find a home to protect yourself from sudden increases. Ask the lender if they offer a free float down if rates go down.
- **Stay informed** about market trends and rate changes.
- **Keep a flexible mindset** about your purchase price or loan type to adapt to changing rates.

7. Inadequate Documentation: Applying for a mortgage requires a lot of paperwork and missing or incomplete documents can delay or derail the process.

How to Overcome It:

- **Create a document checklist** of everything your lender needs (e.g., pay stubs, tax returns, bank statements).
- **Stay organized** by keeping digital copies of your necessary documents.
- **Respond quickly** to any requests for additional information from your lender.

8. Appraisal Issues: An appraisal can sometimes come in lower than the agreed-upon purchase price, complicating your financing.

How to Overcome It:

- **Challenge the appraisal** if you believe it is inaccurate by providing supporting comps or information.

- **Negotiate with the seller** to reduce the price to match the appraised value. The seller may or may not agree; however, it's worth asking.

- **Bring more cash to the table** to make up the difference if you can afford it.

"BELIEVE YOU CAN AND YOU'RE HALFWAY THERE."

- THEODORE ROOSEVELT

Home Sweet Home

9. Unfamiliarity with Loan Types: Many types of loans are available, each with its requirements and benefits. Not knowing which loan is best can make the process overwhelming.

How to Overcome It:

- **Research loan options** (FHA, VA, conventional, ARM (Adjustable-Rate Mortgage) vs. fixed rate) and discuss them with your lender.

- **Ask questions** to ensure you understand the pros and cons of each type of loan.

- **Choose the loan that best fits your long-term financial goals**.

10. Fear of Rejection: The mortgage process can be intimidating, and fear of rejection prevents some buyers from even applying.

How to Overcome It:

- **Get educated** about the mortgage process so you know what to expect.

- **Work closely with a trusted lender** who can guide you through the process and provide honest feedback.

- **Stay positive**: Even if you are not initially approved, you can always take steps to improve your situation and try again. You can also simply try a different lender. Sometimes, it takes talking to three to five or even ten lenders to find the one that is the right fit for you.

Chapter 7 Key Takeaways

- **Monitor Your Credit:** Improve your credit score by paying bills on time, reducing debt, and correcting errors on your credit report.

- **Lower Your Debt-to-Income Ratio:** Reduce debt and explore ways to increase your income or add a co-borrower.

- **Get Prequalified Early:** Know your budget before house hunting to avoid surprises and strengthen negotiations.

- **Stay Organized:** Prepare all necessary documentation to streamline the mortgage process.

- **Be Persistent:** Fear of rejection is normal—work with lenders and take proactive steps to improve your financial standing.

Summary: Applying for a mortgage can feel like navigating a maze of challenges, from low credit scores and high debt-to-income ratios to appraisal issues and interest rate fluctuations. This chapter provides practical strategies to overcome these obstacles, such as improving your credit, saving for a down payment, and staying organized with documentation.

It emphasizes the importance of getting prequalified early, understanding different loan types, and maintaining a positive mindset throughout the process. Whether it is leveraging down payment assistance programs or locking in a favorable interest rate, being proactive and informed will help you secure your dream home. The journey may be complex, but with preparation, persistence, and professional guidance, you can tackle these hurdles and confidently move toward homeownership. Next up, I will discuss credit scores and ideas for getting your scores higher for optimal rates.

Chapter 8

Credit Counts: Building Your Best Score for Home Buying

Let's face it—credit scores are much like report cards for grown-ups. And just like in school, a higher score opens more doors (literally, in this case). Your credit score plays a significant role in whether you can buy a home, the kind of loan you qualify for, and how much you will pay over time. Let's break it down step-by-step to help you build the credit foundation you need.

Why Credit Matters in Home Buying: When you apply for a mortgage, lenders use your credit score to gauge trustworthiness. A higher score means more loan options, better interest rates, and lower costs over time. Conversely, a lower score may limit your options or increase your loan's cost. Here is a general breakdown of credit score ranges:

- **Excellent (740 and above):** You are a lender's dream.

- **Good (700-739):** Solid range; you will get reasonable rates.

- **Fair (650-699):** Loans are possible, but rates could be higher.

- **Poor (600-649):** Approval may be possible, but expect stricter terms.

- **Very Poor (below 600):** Challenging, but not impossible, with proper steps.

For those with lower scores, FHA loans are often a more accessible option due to their leniency with credit requirements.

Why Accuracy Matters: Lenders, landlords, and even some employers use your credit report to assess your reliability. Inaccuracies, such as incorrect personal information or erroneous account details, can lead to misunderstandings or even identity theft. Ensuring your report reflects accurate information is essential for maintaining your financial health.

Check Your Credit: First Steps: Before you even dream of hardwood floors or open-concept kitchens, start by understanding where your credit stands. Your credit report is a snapshot of your financial history, and its accuracy is crucial. Errors in your report could lower your score and jeopardize your ability to secure favorable loan terms.

How to Get Your Free Credit Report: You are entitled to one free credit report annually from each of the three major credit bureaus: Equifax, Experian, and TransUnion. Access them via AnnualCreditReport.com. Get copies of all three reports, check for **errors or discrepancies,** and dispute anything that is incorrect.

1. **Review Personal Information:** Ensure your name, address, Social Security number, and employment history are accurate. Even small errors can cause major complications. It is not uncommon for someone to need to correct their credit report multiple times due to mix-ups with relatives who share the same last name.

2. **Examine Account Details:** Ensure all accounts listed are yours and that the balances, payment histories, and

your status are accurate. Look for unfamiliar accounts or incorrect late payments.

3. **Identify Inaccuracies:** Common errors include duplicate accounts, incorrect balances, or accounts mistakenly attributed to you. Note any discrepancies you find.

4. **Gather Supporting Documents:** Collect documents that support your claim, such as payment records or correspondence with creditors.

5. **Submit a Dispute:** Provide a clear explanation of the error and include copies of supporting documents. You can dispute errors online, by mail, or by phone. Each credit bureau has its own process:

   ○ **Equifax** File a dispute online.

     Website:
     https://www.equifax.com/personal/disputes/

   ○ **Experian** Dispute information.

     Website:
     https://www.experian.com/disputes/main.html

   ○ **TransUnion** Start a dispute.

     Website:
     https://www.transunion.com/credit-disputes

6. **Follow-Up:** The credit bureau typically has 30 days to investigate your dispute. If changes are made, they'll inform you of the outcome and provide a free copy of your updated report.

Top 8 errors frequently found on credit reports:

1. **Incorrect Personal Information:** Errors such as misspelled names, wrong addresses, or inaccurate Social Security numbers.

2. **Accounts That Do Not Belong to You:** Accounts mistakenly attributed to you, possibly due to identity theft or mixed files.

3. **Duplicate Accounts:** The same debt is listed multiple times, which can inflate your perceived debt load.

4. **Incorrect Account Status:** Accounts reported as open when they are closed, or vice versa, or accounts inaccurately marked as delinquent.

5. **Inaccurate Payment History:** Payments were reported late but were actually made on time.

6. **Incorrect Balance or Credit Limit:** Accounts showing incorrect current balances or credit limits affecting your credit utilization ratio.

7. **Outdated Information:** Negative information that should have been removed after the legally required time frame.

8. **Incorrect Public Records:** Errors in public records like bankruptcies or judgments that do not belong to you.

Fixing Errors: Real-Life Example

Take Jane, a young professional from Texas. Despite her strong financial habits, she was denied a mortgage due to several errors on her credit report: a misspelled name, an incorrect address, and a delinquent account that was not hers. Determined to correct this, Jane:

- Accessed her credit reports via AnnualCreditReport.com.

- Identified the errors and gathered supporting documents like bank statements.

- Filed disputes online with each bureau, providing clear explanations.

Within 30 days, the inaccuracies were corrected, her credit score improved, and she secured a favorable mortgage rate to purchase her dream home.

Building Your Credit Foundation: How Mortgage Companies Assist in Repairing Credit

Embarking on the journey to homeownership can be both exciting and daunting, especially when your credit score isn't where it needs to be. A reputable mortgage company can be an invaluable ally in this process. Many top-tier lenders either have in-house credit repair services or partner with specialized credit repair agencies to assist potential homeowners in improving their credit profiles.

These services typically begin with a comprehensive review of your credit report to identify inaccuracies or negative items that may be dragging down your score. Common issues include outdated information, incorrect account details, or even fraudulent activities. By addressing these errors, you should see a significant improvement in your credit score. For instance, credit repair companies work by reviewing and disputing inaccuracies on your credit report, potentially raising your score, but results and timelines can vary.

Beyond correcting errors, these credit repair services offer personalized strategies to enhance your creditworthiness. This might involve guidance on reducing outstanding debts, establishing a history of timely payments, or managing credit utilization effectively. By following a tailored plan, you can work towards achieving a credit score that aligns with mortgage qualification standards.

Moreover, a great mortgage company does not just stop at credit repair. They collaborate with you to set clear, achievable goals on your path to homeownership. This includes outlining the necessary steps, providing timelines, and offering resources to keep you on track. Such structured guidance ensures that you are not navigating the complexities of credit improvement and mortgage qualification alone.

Getting professional advice can help you avoid costly mistakes and sharp dips in your scores. For example, paying off your credit card balance is generally beneficial for your credit score, as it reduces your credit utilization ratio and the amount of credit you are using relative to your total available credit. However, in some cases, you might notice a temporary dip in your credit score after paying off a credit card. If you are trying to buy a home, this could be a costly mistake.

It is important to note that while these services can be highly beneficial, they are not a quick fix. Improving your credit score requires time, discipline, and consistent effort. However, with the support of a dedicated mortgage company and its credit repair partners, you can make informed decisions and take proactive steps toward realizing your dream of homeownership.

In summary, partnering with a mortgage company that offers or collaborates with credit repair services can provide a comprehensive approach to preparing for homeownership. Addressing credit issues and setting clear goals can enhance your financial profile and move you closer to securing the home you've always wanted.

Building Better Credit

Improving your credit takes time and consistent effort, but the rewards are worth it. Here are practical strategies to strengthen your credit profile:

- **Pay On Time:** Set up autopay to avoid missed payments.

- **Low credit utilization**: Use less than 30% of your available credit. Suppose your credit limit is $10,000; it is good to keep your balance under $3,000. If you can keep your utilization under 10%, that would be fantastic and would boost your scores even more.

- **Keep Old Accounts Open:** Length of credit history matters, so do not close old credit cards unnecessarily. (Unless advised to by a loan officer or credit expert)

- **Become an Authorized User:** Ask a trusted family member to add you to their credit card account to benefit from their good credit habits.

Avoid These Common Credit Mistakes

1. **Closing Old Accounts:** Reduces your credit history and can lower your score.

2. **High Credit Utilization:** Signals financial strain; aim to use less than 30% of your available credit.

3. **Ignoring Your Credit Report:** Overlooked errors can cost you points and opportunities.

4. **Late or Missed Payments:** Paying your bills on or before the due date is crucial, as late or missed payments can significantly impact your credit score. If you are paying electronically, aim to make your payment at least five business days in advance to ensure it processes on time. For traditional mail (snail mail), it is best to allow a minimum of two weeks to avoid delays.

5. **Frequent "Hard-Pull" Credit Inquiries**: Too many applications for credit in a short period can negatively affect your score.

Soft Pull vs. Hard Pull: What is the Difference?

- **Soft Pull:** No impact on your credit score. Used for prequalification, background checks, or personal credit inquiries.

- **Hard Pull:** Can lower your score temporarily. Occurs when lenders check your credit for a loan or credit card application.

Real-Life Scenario: The Road to Better Credit

Let's meet Maria. She has been renting for years and is finally ready to buy her first home. When she checks her credit report, she is surprised to find a score of 640—lower than expected. Instead of giving up, Maria takes action:

- She disputes two errors in her report.

- She sets up autopay for her bills and reduces her credit card balances.

- She works with a lender to understand her options and creates a plan.

Six months later, Maria's score is up to 700, and she is prequalified for a mortgage with a better interest rate!

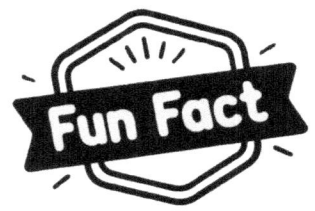

Fun Fact: Over 20% of credit reports contain errors that could impact your score. Checking yours is worth the effort!

1. **Regularly check your credit** report for errors and dispute inaccuracies promptly.

2. Focus on **building strong credit habits**, such as on-time payments and low credit utilization.

3. Seek **professional guidance** from lenders or credit repair services if your score needs improvement.

Summary: Your credit score is a vital part of the home-buying journey, impacting your loan options and costs. Begin by reviewing your credit report, correcting errors, and adopting smart credit habits. With time and effort, you can improve your score, opening the door to better mortgage rates and homeownership opportunities.

With this foundation in place, let's take a closer look at putting together the right team.

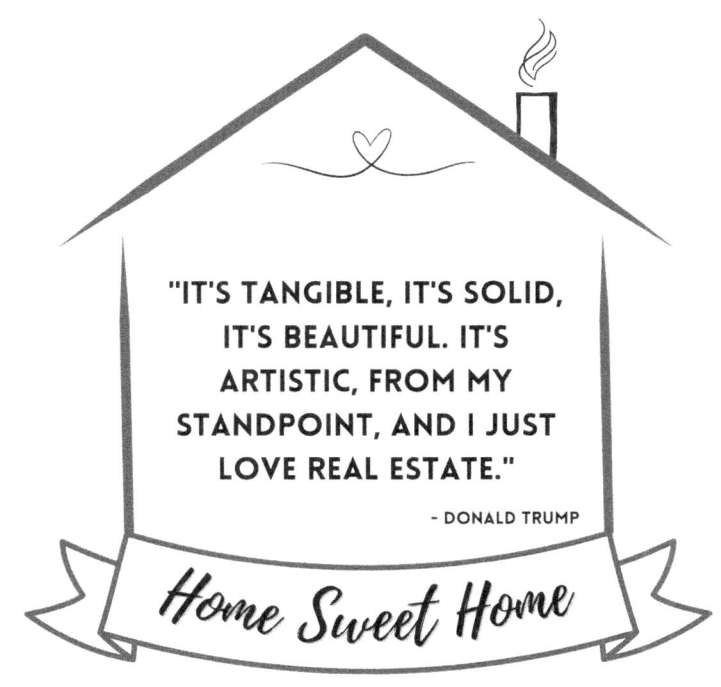

"IT'S TANGIBLE, IT'S SOLID, IT'S BEAUTIFUL. IT'S ARTISTIC, FROM MY STANDPOINT, AND I JUST LOVE REAL ESTATE."

- DONALD TRUMP

Home Sweet Home

Chapter 9

The Homebuying Dream Team: Who You Need and How They Help

Buying a home is not a solo adventure. It is more like a team sport, and you want the best players on your side. Having the right team in place can save you time, money, and stress. Let's break down who you need, why they are essential, and how to choose the right ones.

Do I Need a Real Estate Agent?

The short answer: **Yes, you probably do**. A good real estate agent can be your guide, negotiator, and advocate all rolled into one.

What a Real Estate Agent Does for You

- **Find listings** that meet your criteria.

- **Arranges showings** and provides insight into the pros and cons of each home.

- **Negotiates on your behalf** to get you the best deal possible.

- **Manages paperwork** and ensures all deadlines are met.

Think of an agent as your real estate GPS. They know the area and the market trends and can help steer you clear of potential pitfalls.

Rookie Mistakes a Great
Real Estate Agent Can Help You Avoid

1. **Overpaying** for a home because you are not aware of comparable sales.

2. **Skipping inspections** or waiving contingencies that could protect you.

3. **Getting emotionally attached** to a house that is not a good financial fit.

4. **Ignoring hidden costs**, like property taxes, HOA fees, and insurance.

5. **Failing to Understand Market Trends:** Making an offer without understanding if it is a buyer's or seller's market can lead to overpaying or missing out on a great deal.

6. **Underestimating Closing Costs:** Forgetting to budget for closing costs, such as lender fees, title insurance, and transfer taxes.

7. **Neglecting to Review the Fine Print:** Overlooking key details in contracts or HOA rules that may limit your use of the property.

8. **Overlooking Neighborhood Factors:** Focusing on the house and not considering the areas, neighborhood's amenities, or lack thereof.

9. **Skipping a Preapproval:** Starting the home search without knowing how much you can afford or showing sellers, you are a serious buyer.

10. **Rushing Into Bidding Wars:** Letting emotions drive you to make higher offers than you can comfortably afford.

11. **Not Considering Resale Value:** Ignoring the property's potential resale value could impact your future financial goals.

12. **Overlooking Repair Costs:** Failing to factor in necessary repairs or renovation costs when budgeting.

13. **Missing Out on Incentives:** Not knowing about builder incentives, down payment assistance, or other programs that could save you money.

14. **Failing to Negotiate:** Accepting the first offer or terms without exploring potential savings on price, repairs, or closing costs.

15. **Choosing the Wrong Type of Home:** Focusing on the wrong property type (e.g., single-family home vs. condo) without considering maintenance responsibilities, lifestyle needs, or long-term goals could lead to buyer's remorse.

A skilled real estate agent serves as both a guide and advocate, helping you navigate these pitfalls with confidence. Would you like to elaborate on any of these points?

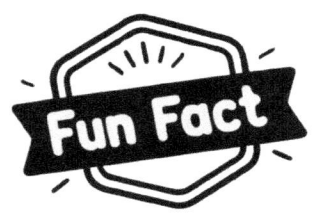 **Fun Fact:** Most real estate agents love house hunting as much as you do. It is like matchmaking, but with homes!

Insights on Negotiating a Buyer Representation Agreement Before You Sign

A **buyer representation agreement** outlines the terms of your relationship with the real estate agent. Here is how to make sure it is fair:

- **Understand the Purpose:** A buyer representation agreement formalizes the relationship between you and your real estate agent, ensuring they represent your best interests during the home-buying process. It is not just paperwork—it is a commitment.

- **Clarify the Commission:** Understand how the agent's commission works. While it is negotiable, often the seller pays the commission, but some agreements include clauses requiring the buyer to cover it under certain circumstances. Confirm this before signing.

- **Understand the terms**: Review the commission structure, contract duration, and obligations.

- **Ask for a shorter term**: If you are unsure about committing, see if the agent will agree to a shorter-term contract. Sometimes, it may even be limited to a showing on one specific property.

- **Know What Services You Will Receive:** Ask your agent what services they'll provide, such as market analysis, negotiation support, property tours, and guidance through closing. This helps set clear expectations.

- **Look for a Cancellation Clause:** Check if the agreement includes a termination or cancellation clause. This allows you to end the agreement if you are unhappy with the agent's service.

- **Check for exclusivity**: Some agreements require you to work only with that agent. Make sure you are comfortable with this commitment.

- **Understand Representation:** If you are calling about a property listed by a specific realtor and they are also showing you the home, be aware that they may represent the seller as a listing agent. Clarify whether they will also act as a dual agent, representing both you and the seller, or if they can refer you to another agent for independent representation to avoid potential conflicts of interest.

What is the Difference Between a Real Estate Agent and a Real Estate Broker?

While both help you buy homes, there is a difference:

- **Real Estate Agent**: Licensed to help clients buy, sell, or rent properties.

- **Real Estate Broker**: Has additional education and can manage other agents. They often oversee transactions and ensure legal compliance.

In short, all brokers are agents, but not all agents are brokers.

"The right guide in your home-buying journey does not just show you houses—they provide clarity, reassurance, and connection. A good realtor helps you make informed decisions that truly feel right."

Brandy Olaniyan, Real Estate Agent

Mortgage Lender or Mortgage Broker: Who is Right for You?

When it comes to securing a mortgage, you will choose between working directly with a **lender** or going through a **mortgage broker**. Understanding their roles, benefits, and potential drawbacks will help you determine which option best suits your needs.

What is a Mortgage Lender? A **lender** is a financial institution or entity that provides funds directly for your mortgage. This includes banks, credit unions, and online lenders. Lenders evaluate your financial profile, approve your loan application, and disburse the funds you need to purchase your home.

Advantages of Using a Lender:

- **Direct Control**: You will work directly with the lender, cutting out intermediaries.

- **Streamlined Process**: Communication is typically straightforward, as there is no middleman.

- **Potentially Lower Costs**: Since lenders do not involve third-party fees, the overall cost may be lower than working with a broker.

When to Choose a Lender (Bank, Credit Union, etc.)

- If your financial situation is straightforward, such as having a steady income, good credit, and no unique financial needs.

- If you prefer to work directly with a single institution to manage the loan process yourself.

- You have stable income, good credit, and straightforward financial circumstances.

What is a Mortgage Broker? A mortgage broker acts as an intermediary between you and multiple lenders. Brokers work on your behalf to shop for loans, find competitive rates, and identify options that match your financial needs. They are particularly useful for borrowers with unique financial circumstances, such as self-employment or low credit scores, as they can find loans tailored to your specific needs.

Advantages of Using a Mortgage Broker:

- **Access to Multiple Lenders**: Brokers can present you with a variety of loan options, including those from lenders you may not have considered.

- **Tailored Solutions**: They can find specialized loan programs, such as Non-QM loans for irregular income, jumbo loans for high-value homes, or loans for borrowers with lower credit scores.

- **Saves Time**: Brokers do the legwork of comparing rates, terms, and lenders, saving you hours, days, or even months of research.

- **Unique Scenarios**: Brokers often work with lenders who are willing to approve loans for borrowers turned down by traditional institutions.

Disadvantages of Using a Mortgage Broker:

- **Additional Fees**: Brokers may charge service fees, which can increase your overall costs. Always ask for a detailed fee breakdown upfront.

- **Potential Conflicts of Interest**: Some brokers may prioritize lenders who offer them higher commissions.

- **Less Direct Control**: Since brokers handle communication with lenders, you rely on them to manage the process efficiently. Be sure to check the broker's reputation and track record, as some loans can fall apart at the last minute if the broker does not have final approval authority or misjudges the lender's requirements. Trustworthy brokers should have strong relationships with reliable lenders.

When to Choose a Mortgage Broker:

- **Unique Financial Circumstances**: If you have fluctuating income, a low credit score, or a history of previous loan denials, a broker can offer tailored solutions.

- **Access to More Options**: If you want access to a broader range of loan programs or need help finding non-traditional financing solutions, brokers can connect you to specialized lenders.

- **Save Time and Effort**: You prefer having someone else handle the legwork of comparing rates and terms across multiple lenders.

- **Turned Down Before?**: If a traditional lender has denied you, a broker can connect you with lenders who specialize in second, third, or even fourth chances, significantly increasing your likelihood of approval.

Specialized Loan Programs Through Brokers: While programs like Jumbo Loans are available through traditional lenders, mortgage brokers often provide greater access to specialized options and lenders for unique situations, making them valuable for non-standard borrowers.

Mortgage brokers often have access to loan programs that traditional lenders might not offer, including:

- **Non-Qualified Mortgages (Non-QM):** For borrowers with unique income situations, such as self-employed individuals or those with irregular income streams.

- **Jumbo Loans:** For properties that exceed conforming loan limits, suitable for high-value home purchases.

- **Interest-Only Loans:** Allowing borrowers to pay only the interest for a set period can benefit specific financial strategies.

- **Loans for Low Credit Scores:** Some brokers work with lenders who are willing to approve loans for borrowers with credit challenges.

- **Been turned down by other Lenders:** Mortgage brokers have access to many lenders, and they may have one that is just the right fit for your needs.

Real-Life Example: How Brokers Can Help

Anna, a freelance graphic designer with inconsistent income, was denied a mortgage by three banks and her credit union. A mortgage broker specializing in loans for self-employed individuals connected Anna with a lender offering a Non-QM loan tailored to her situation. Thanks to the broker's expertise, Anna was able to purchase her dream home.

Best Practice: Consult both lenders and brokers to compare loan terms, rates, and fees. Some of the most creative solutions come from mortgage brokers, as they think outside the box and often have access to unique programs. Plus, brokers aren't always more expensive—many provide competitive rates that rival direct lenders. Always ask for transparency about any additional costs before deciding.

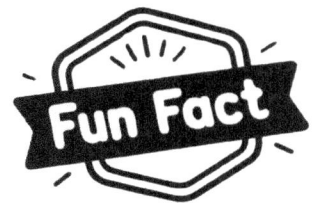

Fun Fact: Did you know that mortgage brokers often have access to over 30 different lenders? That is like having a buffet of loan options compared to the single menu you would get at a bank!

Top Points to Remember

1. **Understand the Difference**: Lenders fund loans directly, while brokers connect you to multiple lenders.

2. **Match to Your Needs**: Choose a lender for simplicity or a broker for tailored solutions and broader options.

3. **Ask Questions**: Always clarify fees, terms, and loan options to make an informed choice.

Remember, the path to homeownership is unique for everyone. By understanding the roles of mortgage lenders and brokers, you can make informed decisions that align with your financial goals and homeownership dreams.

The Essential Guide to Hiring a Home Inspector: Safeguarding Your Investment

Should I hire a home inspector? Yes, yes, and yes! If you buy a pre-owned home, A **home inspector** can uncover potential issues before you commit to buying. If you are buying a new home from a home builder, then you can still hire a home inspector to identify any potential issues before closing.

What to Look for in a Home Inspector

- **Licensed, bonded, and insured**: Ensures you work with a professional who can be held accountable.

- **Experience**: An inspector with years of experience will likely catch subtle issues.

- **Detailed reports**: They should provide a clear report with photos and explanations of the findings.

- **Specialized Knowledge:** If the home has unique features like a pool, septic system, or foundation concerns, look for an inspector with expertise or access to specialists.

- **Recommendations from Trusted Sources:** Ask your real estate agent, friends, or family for recommendations, but make sure to vet the inspector independently to avoid conflicts of interest.

- **Tools and Technology**: Ensure the inspector uses modern tools like thermal imaging, moisture meters, or drones if needed, to provide a more comprehensive evaluation.

What is Included (or Not Included)

- **Included**: Roof, foundation, electrical, plumbing, and HVAC systems.
- **Typically, Not Included**: Cosmetic issues, landscaping, and non-structural details.

Important Note: Do not expect the seller to fix everything on the inspection report. Be prepared to prioritize major repairs, safety concerns, or potential deal-breakers. Do not sweat the small stuff.

The Hidden Danger Beneath:
How a Home Inspection Averted Disaster

When the Thompson family decided to sell their home, they anticipated the usual preparations: decluttering, staging, and minor repairs. However, a startling discovery was made during the buyer's home inspection, which let everyone in the Thompson family know that they were at high risk.

The buyer's home inspector, a seasoned professional, meticulously examined every aspect of their home. Upon inspecting the water heater, he noticed irregular wiring connections. Further investigation revealed that the unit was wired incorrectly, creating a potential hazard that could have led to an explosion.

Understanding the Hazard

Gas water heaters rely on proper electrical connections to function safely. Miswiring can cause components to malfunction, leading to gas leaks or ignition failures. In this case, the incorrect wiring could have caused gas to accumulate, posing a severe explosion risk.

Reflecting on Past Oversights

The Thompsons had lived in the house for years without any apparent issues. Routine maintenance was performed, but they never considered the possibility of such a critical safety concern. This oversight highlighted the importance of thorough inspections by qualified professionals.

The Role of a Professional Home Inspector

A professional home inspector's expertise is invaluable in identifying potential hazards that may not be evident to homeowners. Their comprehensive evaluations cover structural integrity, electrical systems, plumbing, and more, ensuring that both sellers and buyers are aware of any issues.

Taking Immediate Action

Upon learning about the miswiring, the Thompsons promptly hired a licensed electrician to rectify the problem. The faulty wiring was corrected, and the water heater was tested to ensure it operated safely. This swift action not only safeguarded the Thompson family but also maintained the trust of the prospective buyers.

Lessons Learned

This experience underscored the critical importance of safety and the value of professional inspections. Regular maintenance and inspections by qualified professionals are essential to identify and address potential hazards before they escalate.

Top Points to Remember:

- **Prioritize Safety:** Regularly inspect and maintain home systems to prevent potential hazards.

- **Hire Qualified Professionals:** Engage licensed and experienced inspectors and contractors for thorough evaluations and repairs.

- **Stay Informed:** Educate yourself about your home's systems to recognize when professional assistance is needed.

In conclusion, this experience reminds us that unseen dangers can exist in our homes. By prioritizing safety and relying on professional expertise, we can protect our families and ensure our homes remain safe havens.

New vs. Pre-Owned Homes: How Inspections Differ

- **New Homes**: Even with that fresh paint smell, new homes aren't immune to hiccups. Construction slip-ups can sneak in, so it is wise to have an inspection before closing. Most builders offer a one-year warranty covering over 90% of home components. Interestingly, some warranty managers suggest scheduling a third-party inspection around 10-11 months after closing. The house has settled by then, and any quirks are more likely to surface, but they are still within that warranty window.

- **Pre-Owned Homes**: Older homes have character and sometimes a few surprises. Think aging roofs, quirky plumbing, or vintage electrical setups. An inspector can help you uncover these hidden gems (or pitfalls) so you know exactly what you are stepping into.

In both cases, a thorough inspection is your best friend, ensuring your new home is as welcoming as it looks.

The Vintage Home Dilemma:
When Inexperience Costs a Dream

The Miller Family was ready to sell their charming 1920s bungalow, a home full of vintage allure that they knew would captivate the right buyer. The original hardwood floors, intricate moldings, and antique fixtures told stories of a bygone era. However, they also understood that an older home has quirks, especially regarding modern building codes.

Enter the eager first-time buyers, Julia and Tom. They fell in love with the house at first sight, envisioning their future within its historic walls. Their excitement was palpable, and the Millers were thrilled to pass their beloved home to someone who appreciated its character.

Unfortunately, Julia and Tom's real estate agent was relatively new to the field. During the home inspection, the inspector noted several items that, while compliant at the time of construction, didn't align with today's building codes. This included things like the absence of ground fault circuit interrupters (GFCIs) in the kitchen and bathrooms and the use of older electrical wiring methods.

The inspector's report was thorough, as expected. It is their job to point out discrepancies between the home's current state and modern standards, even if those discrepancies are typical for homes of that age. However, the agent, unfamiliar with older properties, interpreted the report as a list of critical flaws. She urgently conveyed this to Julia and Tom, suggesting that the house was fraught with issues.

Understandably, the young couple became anxious. Their dream home now seemed like a potential money pit. Despite the Millers' efforts to explain that these findings were common in older homes and didn't necessarily indicate serious problems,

Julia and Tom's confidence was shaken. They decided to withdraw their offer, fearing unforeseen expenses and safety concerns.

A few weeks later, the Millers received an offer from an unexpected source—A home inspector. With years of experience evaluating properties, he recognized that the so-called "issues" were typical for a house of its age and didn't pose significant concerns. He appreciated the home's character and saw its true value, making a fair offer that the Millers gladly accepted.

Top Points to Remember:

- **Understand the Context of Inspection Reports**: In older homes, certain features may not meet current codes but are not necessarily problematic. It is essential to distinguish between genuine issues and standard characteristics of vintage properties.

- **Choose Experienced Professionals:** Working with real estate agents and inspectors with experience with older homes or any specific home type you seek can provide valuable insights and prevent misunderstandings.

- **Communicate Openly:** Discuss concerns with all parties involved if they arise from an inspection. Understanding the nature of the findings can help make informed decisions.

Ultimately, the Miller Family's bungalow found a new owner who cherished its history and charm. Julia and Tom, disappointed, eventually settled on a different house. This experience highlights the importance of expertise and clear communication in real estate transactions, ensuring buyers and sellers can confidently move forward.

"Owning a home is an investment in your future. It builds equity and creates a foundation for financial stability. It is not just a purchase; it is a step toward long-term growth."

Mary Ann Juarez, Real Estate Agent
Ziglar Realty

Tax Advisor or Accountant:
An Optional Yet Helpful Addition

A **tax advisor or accountant** can help you understand the tax implications and benefits of buying a home. The information below is for educational purposes and to help you know what questions to ask. Everyone's situation is different, so be sure to consult your tax advisor about your specific situation.

"OWNING A HOME IS A KEYSTONE TO WEALTH BOTH FINANCIAL AFFLUENCE AND EMOTIONAL SECURITY."

- SUZE ORMAN

Home Sweet Home

How They Help

- **Tax benefits**: They'll explain deductions like mortgage interest and property taxes.

- **Long-term planning**: They can help you understand how owning a home affects your overall financial plan.

While not essential, a tax advisor can be valuable, especially if this is your first time buying a home.

Owning a home isn't just about having a place to call your own; it also comes with several tax benefits that can make a significant difference in your financial picture. Let's break down some of the key advantages.

1. Mortgage Interest Deduction

One of the most substantial tax perks for homeowners is the ability to deduct mortgage interest. If you itemize your deductions, you can subtract the interest paid on your mortgage from your taxable income. If you are married and filing jointly for loans taken out after December 15, 2017, you may be able to deduct interest on the first $750,000 of mortgage debt. This deduction can lead to considerable savings, especially in the early years of your mortgage when interest payments are higher.

2. Property Tax Deduction

Homeowners can also deduct state and local property taxes, up to a combined total of $10,000 per year. This deduction is particularly beneficial in areas with high property taxes, helping to reduce your overall tax liability.

3. Capital Gains Exclusion

When you sell your primary residence, you may be able to exclude a significant portion of the profit from capital gains tax. If you've owned and lived in the home for at least two of the five years before the sale, you may be able to exclude up to $250,000 of gain if you are single or up to $500,000 if you are married filing jointly. This exclusion can be a substantial benefit when it is time to move on to your next home.

4. Mortgage Insurance Deduction

If your down payment was less than 20%, you might be paying for private mortgage insurance (PMI) or mortgage insurance premiums (MIP). The good news is that, subject to income limitations, these premiums may be deductible, further reducing your taxable income.

5. Home Office Deduction

For self-employed people who use part of their home exclusively for business, the home office deduction allows you to deduct expenses related to that portion of your home. This can include a percentage of utilities, insurance, and even depreciation. However, it is essential to meet specific IRS requirements to qualify.

6. Energy Efficiency Credits

Making energy-efficient improvements to your home can qualify you for tax credits. For example, installing solar panels or energy-efficient windows may provide credits that directly reduce your tax bill. These incentives not only save you money on taxes but also reduce your energy bills.

A Quick Anecdote

Consider Jane, a first-time homeowner who purchased her home with a $300,000 mortgage at a 4% interest rate. In her first year, she paid approximately $11,900 in mortgage interest. By itemizing her deductions, she could deduct this amount, reducing her taxable income and saving her a significant sum on her taxes. Additionally, she deducted $5,000 in property taxes, further enhancing her tax savings.

Top Points to Remember:

- **Itemize Deductions:** To take advantage of these benefits, you must itemize your deductions rather than taking the standard deduction.

- **Keep Records:** Maintain thorough records of all mortgage interest payments, property taxes, and qualifying expenses throughout the year.

- **Consult a Professional:** Tax laws can be complex and subject to change. Consulting with a tax professional can help ensure you are maximizing your benefits.

In conclusion, homeownership offers several tax advantages that can lead to substantial savings. By understanding and utilizing these benefits, you can make your home an even more valuable investment.

Insuring Your Assets: Protecting Your Investment

Homeowners insurance is non-negotiable when buying a home, but there is more to insuring your assets than just fire and theft coverage. This is often referred to as Hazard Insurance.

Types of Coverage

- **Basic homeowners insurance**: Covers damage from fire, theft, and certain natural disasters.

- **Flood insurance**: Why might a house need flood insurance? If FEMA designates your home in a high-risk flood zone (at least a **1% annual chance of flooding** (commonly referred to as a "100-year floodplain"), flood insurance is usually required with a federally backed mortgage. Standard homeowners' insurance will not cover flood damage, and even homes outside these zones can flood. This type of insurance is not automatic, so if you are in a flood zone or just want flood insurance for extra peace of mind, ask your insurance agent about this.

- **Title insurance**: Protection against financial loss from defects in the property's title. (more on this later)

Be sure to shop around for a reputable, dependable homeowners insurance company with fair rates and understand exactly what is covered (and what isn't).

Top 10 Questions to Ask When Getting Homeowner Insurance

1. **What does the policy cover?** Understand the basics of your policy, including protection for the home's structure, personal belongings, liability, and additional living expenses. Do you need any additional riders for specific valuables?

2. **What is not covered by the policy?** Ask about exclusions like floods, earthquakes, or specific wear-and-tear damages, and consider additional coverage if needed.

3. **How much coverage do I need?** Ensure the policy covers the full cost to rebuild your home, not just its market value, and adequately protects your belongings.

4. **What is the deductible?** Find out how much you will pay out of pocket before insurance covers a claim and whether different deductibles apply to specific events (e.g., wind or hail damage). Ask for a quote with higher or lower deductibles to compare rates and then decide what is best for you based on your risk tolerance.

5. **Are there discounts available?** Inquire about discounts for installing security systems, bundling insurance

policies, being claim-free, having excellent credit, or making any specific home improvements.

6. **What is the claims process like?** Learn how to file a claim, how long it takes to resolve claims, and whether the company has a good reputation for customer service.

7. **Does the policy cover replacement cost or actual cash value?** Replacement cost reimburses for new items, while actual cash value factors in depreciation, resulting in much lower payouts.

8. **How are natural disasters covered?** Ask about specific coverage for risks common in your area, such as hurricanes, tornados, floods, wildfires, or earthquakes, and whether additional policies are necessary.

9. **Are there coverage limits for high-value items?** Determine if you need extra protection for expensive belongings like jewelry, art, antiques, or electronics that may exceed policy limits.

10. **Does the policy include liability coverage?** Liability coverage protects you if someone is injured on your property or if you cause damage to someone else. For example, it can cover medical bills if a guest trips on your walkway or repairs if your tree damages a neighbor's fence. Most policies include $100,000 to $300,000 in coverage but review the amount to ensure it is enough to protect your assets. If needed, consider an umbrella policy for extra liability protection. Verify the amount of liability protection for accidents or injuries on your property and consider whether it is sufficient.

Top Points to Remember

Putting together your home-buying Dream Team is one of the most important steps in the process. From the real estate agent who shows you the best listings to the lender who secures your mortgage, each team member plays a vital role in getting you to the finish line.

Think of your team as the Avengers of real estate; they all have different skills, but when combined, they make you unstoppable. So, assemble your dream team, ask the right questions, and get ready to conquer the home-buying process!

While homeownership offers various tax benefits, it is essential to recognize that individual circumstances can significantly influence the advantages you may receive. Factors such as income level, filing status, and specific financial situations play a crucial role. Therefore, consulting with a Certified Public Accountant (CPA) or a qualified tax professional is highly recommended to understand how these benefits apply to your unique situation. They can provide personalized advice, ensuring you make informed decisions that align with your financial goals and comply with current tax laws.

The title company is critical in ensuring your home purchase is legally sound. They perform a thorough title search to verify the property's ownership history and ensure there are no outstanding liens, claims, or disputes that could jeopardize your ownership. The title company also issues title insurance, which protects you and your lender from potential legal challenges to the property's ownership. At closing, they coordinate document signing, exchange funds, and ensure the transaction is finalized smoothly. **In the Chapter called: "Closing: Wrapping Up Your New Home Purchase,"** learn more about the title company's role and closing attorney!

Teamwork Makes the Dream Work: Your Home-Buying Partners

When Emma and Liam decided to buy their first home, they felt like explorers venturing into uncharted territory. The excitement was evident, but so was their uncertainty. They quickly realized that much like assembling a crack team for a heist movie (minus the crime), buying a home requires a group of experts to guide you through the process.

"NOW IS THE VERY BEST TIME TO BUY A HOUSE..."

- UNKNOWN

Home Sweet Home

Key Insights From The Experts

Gaylene Rogers Lonergan
A Real Estate & Title Attorney

Since the first time, homebuyers have never been through the home purchase process before, and they are somewhat at the mercy of the professionals who are handling their closings/sales. That means that they have to put their trust in the mortgage brokers, real estate agents, title agents, and sellers (who have been through this process before). Oftentimes, many do not feel that they have anyone looking out for their particular best interest. So, as a real estate and title attorney who has practiced for over 40 years, I compiled a list of concerns that first-time buyers need to be aware of and ensure are handled correctly.

First, make sure that you understand everything that is covered in your purchase contract. My best advice is to retain legal representation to review everything on your behalf and advise you what you are obligating yourself to prior to executing the contract. This cost should not be more than $500 or less. Do not just assume that the agent, mortgage broker, or title agent handles this for you. Once the contract is signed, then it is really too late. This is particularly true on new build contracts with a builder. These contracts can be quite extensive, and the terms may not be in the buyer's favor. Keep in mind that with large builders, their standard contracts are often non-negotiable. However, certain items and incentives may still be up for discussion. It is crucial to fully understand what you are agreeing to before signing.

Second, once the contract is signed and put into the title company's escrow, then there are a number of items that need to be provided/reviewed before closing. These include:

1. **Title Commitment** – this is the report regarding the current state of the title to the property prepared by a professional title examiner. This report shows what currently affects the property and what must be resolved in order for the buyer to receive an acceptable clear title to the property. If you do not understand anything contained in the title commitment, speak to an independent party to go over it with you in order to make sure there are no surprises.

2. **Survey** - a survey is a drawing regarding the property containing all improvements, easements, setbacks, etc., affecting the property. There may be encroachments of improvements over easement lines, setback lines, or boundary lines that must be addressed before closing. It is acceptable to allow a seller to provide an existing survey, provided that the title company accepts it for insuring purposes and the seller provides an affidavit stating that there have been NO CHANGES since the survey was done and certified. I also recommend paying the small premium required to have the title company ensure the accuracy of the survey in the title policy.

3. **Home Owner Association Documents** – Most new subdivisions being built will be subject to restrictions and other matters governed by a homeowner's association. Always get these documents provided to you PRIOR to closing for review. These documents include a Declaration of Restrictions, Covenants, and Easements,

as well as a Resale Certificate issued by the Homeowners Association. The Declaration needs to be reviewed so you know exactly what restrictions on the uses of your property are in existence, i.e., nature of improvements, color, landscaping, etc. The Resale Certificate will tell you whether there are any current violations of the Restrictions or Bylaws of the Association and how much the dues and other costs will be for the buyer.

4. **Taxes** – A tax certificate is required for closing by the title company. This document shows the current state of the payment of property taxes and what exemptions are currently in place. This is essential that the new homebuyer knows what the taxes are, what exemptions affect the property, and what the future taxes could be. There are a number of issues involving taxes:

   a. Purchasing a property from an over-65 seller – the over-65 seller may have an exemption that the new buyer will not be entitled to this can change the total taxes due the following years and the escrow payments that may be required under the new mortgage loan.

   b. Purchasing a property from the heirs of an over 65 deceased owner – the Over 65 exemption goes away the day the deceased owner passes away. There is no more entitlement to that tax reduction; however, the tax office has no way of knowing that an owner has passed away until a document is recorded in the real property records or court records, i.e., a probate of a will, an affidavit of heirship, etc. Once these documents are recorded, the tax office will eventually go back and reassess the taxes for the period of time since the deceased owner's death – if the buyer is not careful, they could be saddled with those reassessed taxes post-closing. AND this reassessment is not covered by the title policy issued to the buyer by the title company at closing.

c. Purchasing a newly constructed property from a builder – the assessed value for taxes for the prior year, pre-completion, will be significantly lower than the assessed value of the property once the improvements are constructed.

d. Purchasing a newly constructed property that is part of previously undeveloped land – the issue of "rollback taxes" can come into play in this scenario, and the buyer could end up owing the prior year's taxes based upon a prior exemption.

5. **Prorations** - the contract will call for taxes to be prorated between the parties, i.e., the seller should be responsible for the portion of the year that the property was owned by the seller, and the buyer should be responsible for the portion of the year after closing. The title company calculates these prorations at the closing; however, the issues brought up in Item 4 above can come into play with prorations as well. Not all escrow agents may be knowledgeable in these issues, and the chance of errors in the prorations (to the buyer's detriment) can be high in certain instances.

6. **Post-closing** – as the buyer, make sure you receive the original Owner Policy of Title Insurance from the title company. It should come in the mail no later than six to eight weeks following closing. This is your insurance policy regarding the state of the title to the property. It should be placed in your records regarding the property so you can access it if any issues regarding the title develop. If you do not receive it, follow up with your title closing office until it is received.

7. **Carefully Choose Your Closing Agent:** As a closing agent who has handled thousands of transactions of all types, I can tell you that title companies and agents vary widely in their expertise and approach. Some are streamlined for efficiency, focusing solely on standard, straightforward transactions and often lacking the flexibility to handle unique situations. Others specialize in a broad range of deals, including investor loans, hard-money loans, and creative financing. It is essential to choose a team with the right experience, especially if your transaction requires out-of-the-box solutions. Be sure that you are comfortable that the professionals you are dealing with understand your transaction and the various issues that can arise.

My last tip – if you do not understand anything along the entire process, do not hesitate to ask questions and if you can afford it, seek your own professional advice from a lawyer who can represent you on all these concerns.

Gaylene Rogers Lonergan
Lonergan Law Firm PLLC
Dallas, Texas

The Conductor of Your Homebuying Orchestra

Bringing Together

- Loan Officers
- Sellers
- Title Companies
- Insurance Company

- Home Inspector
- Mortgage Company
- Appraiser
- Closing Agent

Harmonizing Your Home Search:
The Realtor's Role as Conductor

We've covered a lot of ground in this book so far. Are you feeling a bit overwhelmed? Do not worry! You do not need to be an expert on everything. The goal is that you now have a solid foundation and plenty of ideas to ask the right questions. Great News! In the home-buying process, a realtor acts as the conductor of an orchestra, harmonizing various elements to create a seamless experience. They coordinate with lenders, inspectors, appraisers, and other professionals, ensuring each component aligns perfectly. By managing these relationships and overseeing the intricate details, realtors guide buyers smoothly from the initial search to the final closing, making the complex journey of purchasing a home more manageable and efficient.

Imagine you are attending a symphony without a conductor. The musicians, though talented, might play out of sync, creating a clamoring racket instead of beautiful harmony. In the home-buying process, your real estate agent serves as the conductor, orchestrating each element, from negotiations to inspections, to ensure a seamless and harmonious experience.

A professional realtor isn't just someone who unlocks doors for showings; they are the conductor of a well-orchestrated symphony, ensuring each note of your home-buying journey hits the right pitch. They've often spent years cultivating relationships with mortgage lenders, home inspectors, appraisers, and title companies. Their network isn't just a Rolodex of names; it is a curated list of trusted professionals who have proven their value time and again.

Take, for instance, the mortgage lender who can demystify the maze of loan options, guiding you to the one that best fits your financial tune. Or the home inspector who does not just glance at the roof but knows to check that quirky attic space where squirrels might be hosting their annual jamboree. And let's not forget the title company that ensures the property's history is as clean as a whistle, so you do not inherit any unexpected 'guests' in the form of liens or disputes.

By working with an experienced realtor's dream team, you are not just saving time—you are avoiding costly mistakes and ensuring a smoother journey. Think of it as tuning into a beautiful symphony, where the expert handles every detail, allowing you to focus on enjoying the process. When your realtor says, "I have got someone for that," trust that you are in the hands of a skilled conductor, orchestrating a peaceful and harmonious home-buying experience.

"When you are trying to buy a house without the help of a realtor, know that you are the underdog!"

Hiwot Melaku, Realtor/Broker

The Tale of Two Homebuyers: A Guide to Choosing the Right Real Estate Team

Emma's Success with an Expert Realtor

Emma, a first-time buyer, hired Susan, a seasoned real estate agent. Susan guided Emma through every step, from securing pre-approval to closing. She introduced Emma to trusted professionals, including a mortgage broker and inspector, and helped negotiate repairs, saving Emma thousands. With Susan's expertise, Emma closed smoothly and moved into her dream home without issues.

Jake's Struggles with an Inattentive Agent

Jake hired Tom, an inexperienced agent, and faced numerous challenges. Tom didn't stress the importance of pre-approval, causing Jake to lose his first offer. Goerge, the home inspector that Jake himself because he was the cheapest inspector, missed significant structural problems, leading to costly repairs. Poor negotiation and mismanagement during closing left Jake stressed and regretting his choice of relator.

Top Points to Remember

1. **Choose Wisely**: A skilled and seasoned agent can save you time, money, and stress.
2. **Value the Network:** Agents with reliable connections add immense value.
3. **Communicate Effectively:** Clear, proactive communication from your agent ensures smoother transactions.
4. **Stay Involved:** While your team provides guidance, staying engaged ensures your needs are met.

Common Mistakes to Avoid

- **Skipping Pre-Approval**: Without it, you risk losing your dream home.

- **Settling for the Wrong Agent**: By working with an experienced realtor's dream team, you are avoiding costly mistakes and ensuring a smoother journey. A great agent listens to your needs, communicates clearly, and guides you confidently. If you feel pressured or the process feels chaotic, it might be a sign they are not the right fit. The right agent ensures your home-buying experience hits all the right notes.

- **Choosing the Cheapest Inspector**: Always vet inspectors and read all documents carefully. And remember, saving a few dollars now on the inspection costs could cost you thousands of dollars in the future.

By surrounding yourself with experienced professionals, you can avoid costly mistakes and navigate the home-buying process with confidence, just like Emma did. Up next: A deeper dive into assembling the right home-buying team!

Chapter 9 Key Takeaways

- **Your Realtor as the Conductor**: A skilled realtor is a key player in your home-buying journey, coordinating with lenders, inspectors, appraisers, and title companies to ensure a smooth process.
- **Choose the Right Team**: Surround yourself with experienced professionals, including a trusted realtor, mortgage lender or broker, title company, a skilled home inspector, etc. can help to avoid costly mistakes.
- **Stay Involved:** While your team handles the heavy lifting, staying informed and asking questions ensures your needs are met.
- **Avoid Common Mistakes**: Skipping pre-approval, choosing the wrong professionals, and failing to communicate effectively can lead to unnecessary stress and financial losses.

Summary: Buying a home is a team effort, and assembling the right "dream team" is essential for a successful and stress-free experience. Your realtor acts as the conductor, orchestrating the various players—including lenders, inspectors, and title companies—to create a seamless process. Each team member plays a crucial role in helping you avoid pitfalls, save money, and ensure your home-buying journey is as smooth as possible. By working with experienced professionals, negotiating clear agreements, and staying involved, you can confidently navigate the path to homeownership. With the right team, you are not just buying a house; you are creating a harmonious experience that leads to your dream home.

In the following chapter, we will explore "Rookie Mistakes."

Chapter 10

Rookie Mistakes – What First-Time Homebuyers Should Watch Out For

Buying your first home is a thrilling adventure, but it is also a complex process where mistakes can be costly. The good news? By learning from the experiences of others, you can avoid common pitfalls that might derail your journey. This chapter is not about rehashing everything you have already read—it is about focusing on the most critical mistakes first-time buyers make and how to steer clear of them, which can save you thousands of dollars, reduce stress, and give you peace of mind throughout your journey to homeownership.

1. Skipping Mortgage Pre-Approval

- **Why It is a Rookie Mistake**: Failing to get pre-approved for a mortgage means you are shopping blind. You might fall in love with a home you cannot afford or miss out on opportunities in a competitive market.

- **The Consequences**: Without pre-approval, sellers may not take your offer seriously, and you risk delays when the perfect home comes along.

- **How to Avoid It**:
    - Start early, even if you are not ready to buy yet.
    - Work with a reputable lender to create a SMART (Specific, Measurable, Achievable, Relevant, Time-bound) plan tailored to your financial situation.

2. Buying an Over-Improved House

- **Why It is a Rookie Mistake**: An over-improved home might look like a dream, but its luxury upgrades could make it difficult to sell later. If the home's value exceeds what is typical for the neighborhood, future buyers may not pay for those high-end features.

- **The Consequences**: You could overpay for a property and struggle to recoup your investment when it is time to sell.

- **How to Avoid It**:

  - Focus on location over luxury—upgrades can be added, but the neighborhood is permanent.

  - Compare the home's features to those of others in the area.

  - Think long-term: prioritize improvements that add value, like a new roof or updated HVAC system, over purely aesthetic upgrades.

3. Not Hiring Professionals

- **Why It is a Rookie Mistake**: Some buyers think they can handle the process solo to save money, but real estate transactions involve complexities that are easy to overlook.

- **The Consequences**: Without professional guidance, you might miss red flags during inspections, overpay, or get stuck in a contract that does not favor you.

- **How to Avoid It**:

  - **Hire a Real Estate Agent**: Your agent orchestrates the entire process, from negotiating offers to coordinating inspections. Choose one with deep local expertise.

  - **Work with a Home Inspector**: A good inspector identifies potential issues that could cost you down the road.

  - **Select a Trusted Lender**: Your lender secures financing and helps you navigate mortgage options.

Pro Insight: Even if it seems costly, skipping inspections or expert advice could cost you far more in the long run.

4. Not Asking Questions

- **Why It is a Rookie Mistake**: First-time buyers often feel embarrassed to ask questions, but staying silent can lead to misunderstandings and missed opportunities.

- **The Consequences**: Critical details about the property or process might be overlooked, leaving you unprepared for potential challenges.

- **How to Avoid It**:

  - **Be Curious**: Ask about the home's systems (roof age, HVAC condition, past repairs), the neighborhood, and the buying process.

- Write Down Questions: Keep a running list so you do not forget anything during showings or meetings.

- Stay Engaged: Your agent, lender, and inspector are there to help—use their expertise!

5. Overextending Your Budget

- **Why It is a Rookie Mistake**: Just because you are approved for a large loan does not mean you should spend the maximum amount.

- **The Consequences**: Stretching your finances can lead to stress and sacrifices in other areas of your life.

- **How to Avoid It**:
  - Set a realistic budget based on your lifestyle and future goals.
  - Consider trade-offs: Will this home mean cutting vacations or dining out? Make sure the sacrifice is worth it.

6. Waiving the Home Inspection

- **Why It is a Rookie Mistake**: In competitive markets, some buyers waive inspections to make their offer more appealing—but this is risky.

- **The Consequences**: Skipping an inspection could leave you with unexpected and costly repairs after closing.

- **How to Avoid It**:
  - Never Skip It Entirely: Always retain the right to an inspection.
  - Cap Repair Requests: Offer to limit requests to significant issues to stay competitive.

- ○ **Consider a Pre-Inspection**: Schedule an inspection before making your offer to avoid contingencies.

- ○ **Request "Information Only" Inspections**: Get the inspection for your knowledge without renegotiating the deal.

- ○ **Review Seller's Reports**: If available, ask for the seller's inspection report and have it reviewed by your inspector.

A professional inspection is a small cost compared to the potential expense of major repairs. Stay informed and protect your investment.

7. Ignoring Resale Value

- **Why It is a Rookie Mistake**: It is easy to fall in love with a quirky home but consider that features that appeal to you may not attract future buyers.

- **The Consequences**: You may face additional costs to make the home marketable when it is time to sell.

- **How to Avoid It**: Prioritize features with broad appeal, like good location, functional layout, and practical upgrades.

8. Underestimating Closing Costs

- **Why It is a Rookie Mistake**: Many buyers focus on the down payment and forget about closing costs, which typically range from 2% to 5% of the purchase price.

- **The Consequences**: Failing to budget for these expenses can cause financial stress at closing.

- **How to Avoid It**: Budget for closing costs early and request a detailed estimate from your lender and title company.

9. Forgetting About Maintenance Costs

- **Why It is a Rookie Mistake**: Homeownership does not end with the purchase—it includes ongoing maintenance and repairs.

- **The Consequences**: Unexpected expenses can strain your budget.

- **How to Avoid It**: Set aside 1% to 2% of the home's value annually for maintenance.

10. Letting Emotions Rule

- **Why It is a Rookie Mistake**: Falling in love with a home can cloud your judgment, leading to poor financial decisions.

- **The Consequences**: You might overpay or overlook critical flaws.

- **How to Avoid It**: Balance emotions with logic. Ensure the home fits your budget and long-term goals.

Chapter 10 Key Takeaways

Avoiding rookie mistakes can save you money, reduce stress, and help you make a confident home purchase. Here is what to remember:

1. **Get Pre-Approved**: Start with a SMART financial plan and pre-approval to set yourself up for success.

2. **Hire Professionals**: Surround yourself with a trusted team to guide you through the process.

3. **Ask Questions**: Stay curious and proactive to avoid surprises.

4. **Stick to Your Budget**: Buy within your means to maintain financial stability.

5. **Think Long-Term**: Choose a home that meets your current needs and future goals.

Summary: With the right preparation and mindset, you will avoid costly pitfalls and enjoy the journey to homeownership. When you finally step through the front door of your first home, you will know it was all worth it!

With this foundation in place, we're ready to explore closing on your new home and what that looks like

Chapter 11

Closing: Wrapping Up Your Home Purchase

You have made it! After searching for homes, securing financing, and negotiating the terms, you can make it official and wrap up your home purchase with a large, beautiful bow. This step is often referred to as **closing**. This is where you finalize the purchase and, finally, get the keys to your

new home. While the closing day is exciting, it can also seem overwhelming. A little preparation will help it go smoothly.

Title Insurance and Title Company Fees

Title Insurance: Title insurance protects you and your lender against potential disputes or defects in the property's title. It ensures that you will not face financial loss due to past ownership issues, liens, or claims.

Title Company Fees: These fees cover services such as conducting a title search, releasing liens, transfer of monies funding the transactions and handling the paperwork necessary for a smooth transaction. Common costs include settlement fees, document preparation fees, legal recording fees, and title search fees, all essential for securely finalizing your home purchase.

What is a Title Company or Closing Attorney, and What is Their Role?

A title company or closing attorney ensures the legal and financial aspects of your home purchase are completed accurately and efficiently. Their key responsibilities include:

- Verifying that the property's title is free of liens or disputes and can be legally transferred to you.

- Managing the closing process by preparing and reviewing documents, facilitating the signing of final paperwork, and distributing funds to the appropriate parties.

Regional Differences:

- In states like Texas and California, title companies handle most closing tasks.

- In states like Georgia or South Carolina, a closing attorney is required to oversee the transaction. (Consult local experts to understand normal practices in your area)

Regardless of the approach, their ultimate goal is to protect your ownership rights and ensure the transaction is legally binding. To avoid surprises, ask your real estate agent about local practices so you will know what to expect.

Title Insurance: A Safety Net for the Past and Future
Think of title insurance as a time machine—it protects you from problems rooted in the property's past, allowing you to enjoy a secure future. Real estate laws and norms vary and evolve, so always consult local experts for the most up-to-date guidance.

Who Pays for the Title Company or Closing Attorney?

The cost of a title company or closing attorney is typically negotiated between the buyer and seller and often varies by location. In some areas, the **buyer** is expected to cover the fees; in others, it is the **seller** who pays or sometimes the costs are split between both parties. For example, in Texas, sellers usually pay for the title policy. It is essential to clarify who pays what during negotiations and review the purchase agreement to understand who is responsible. Always consult your real estate agent or attorney for guidance based on local customs.

Who Chooses the Title Company or Closing Attorney?

The choice of a title company or closing attorney typically depends on local customs and the negotiation between the buyer and seller. In some areas, the buyer selects the title company, while in others, the seller chooses since they are covering the costs of the title insurance policy. In almost all instances, the choice of the title company is negotiable between the parties. Often, the decision is highly influenced by a recommendation from the realtor, who can suggest a trusted title company to help ensure a smooth transaction. Regardless of who selects it, both parties should ensure the chosen company or attorney is reputable, experienced, and familiar with local laws.

What to Expect at Closing

Closing is the process where ownership is transferred from the seller to you. **It is the moment you become an official homeowner.** And YES, it is ok to jump up and down with joy!

How Long Does Closing Take?

- For pre-owned homes or completed new builds, closing typically occurs 30-45 days after your offer is accepted (meaning you have your future home under contract), though this timeline can vary depending on the circumstances. If you are building a house with a builder, ask for their estimated closing date, but remember that constructing a new home is not an exact science. With a new home that you are building or is still under construction, it is normal for the closing date to shift either earlier or later than expected.

- Delays may occur due to loan approvals, appraisal issues, construction, repairs, or numerous other factors. So, to avoid chaos, the best practice is NOT to schedule moving trucks until after closing.

Working with a Title Company: Key Tips and Must-Checks

- **Verify Ownership History:** Ensure the title company conducts a thorough title search to confirm there are no liens, disputes, or ownership issues that could affect your purchase.

- **Review the Title Commitment:** Carefully read the title commitment document to understand any exceptions, exclusions, or unresolved issues in the title.

- **Understand Title Insurance:** Confirm the type of title insurance you are purchasing and what it covers—both the lenders and owner's policies—and ensure you are adequately protected. Yes, you want both lender's and owner's policies!

- **Check the Legal Description:** Ensure the property's legal description matches what you are purchasing, especially if the property includes acreage or multiple parcels.

- **Request Timely Updates:** Stay in touch with the title company throughout the process to ensure there are no delays or unresolved issues before closing day.

- **Understand HOA Dues and Rules:** The title company often provides a disclosure packet if the property is in an HOA. Review it for rules, fees, and restrictions.

- **Review Your Closing Disclosure:** Compare the final closing disclosure from the title company with your loan estimate to ensure all costs align with what was promised by your lender.

These insights will help you navigate the title company process with confidence and avoid unexpected hiccups during your home-buying journey!

Preparing for Closing: Your Pre-Closing Checklist

Getting everything ready before the closing day is essential. Here is what to do:

1. Review the Closing Disclosure

- You should typically receive a **Closing Disclosure** at least three days before closing. It outlines your final loan terms, monthly payments, and closing costs.

- Compare it to your initial Loan Estimate to check for unexpected changes.

- This is all very time-sensitive, so if possible, review it and ask any questions on the same day you receive it.

2. Conduct a Final Walkthrough

- A final walkthrough of your new home usually takes place within 24 hours of closing.

- Ensure the home is in the same condition as agreed upon and that any promised repairs are complete.

- If you find any issues, inform your real estate agent right away.

3. Gather Required Documents

- Bring a **government-issued ID**, your Closing Disclosure, proof of homeowner's insurance, and any other documents your lender requests.

- Have a **certified check** or arrange a **wire transfer** for your closing costs and down payment.

  - **Beware of Wire Fraud: Protect Your Funds:** Wire fraud is a serious risk during real estate transactions. Always double-check wire instructions by calling the title company or closing attorney directly using a verified phone number, not one from an email. Never send funds without confirming the details to avoid falling victim to scammers.

"OUR HOME IS OUR CASTLE, OUR SANCTUARY, OUR HAVEN OF SAFETY. IT IS WHERE WE CAN JUST BE, CREATE, AND ENJOY THE PLEASURES OF LIFE."
- JEWEL STAR

Home Sweet Home

What Are Closing Costs?

Closing costs are the fees required to complete the purchase. They generally range from **2% to 5% of the purchase price** (not including Real Estate agent fees).

Common Closing Costs

- **Items you typically pay for before closing might include:**
    - **Appraisal Fee:** The cost of a professional appraisal to determine the property's market value, required by lenders to ensure the loan amount is appropriate.

- Home Inspection Fee: The expense of hiring a home inspector to evaluate the property's condition and identify potential issues.

- **Items that are commonly paid at the closing table:**
  - **Loan Processing & origination fee**: Charged by the lender for processing the loan.
  - **Title Insurance and Title Company Fees**
  - **Prepaid Property Taxes and Insurance**: These are often collected at closing and held in an escrow account with your mortgage company's servicer.
  - **HOA:** If your home is in a Homeowners Association, you may have a transfer or other miscellaneous fees as well as monthly or quarterly payments.
  - **Prepaid Interest**: Covers the interest on your loan from the closing date to the end of the month.
  - **Mortgage Insurance**: If your down payment is less than 20%, this initial premium may be due at closing (consult your lender for details).

Helpful Hint: Be mindful that practices can vary by area, so ask questions! Always request a breakdown of closing costs from your lender ahead of time to avoid surprises.

Who Will Be at the Closing Table?

- **Mandatory Attendees**
  - **You**: This means everyone who is buying the home must sign. You are the star of the show! Be ready to sign a lot of documents.

- ○ **Closing agent**: From a title company or attorney who facilitates the process.
- **Optional Attendees**
  - ○ **Your real estate agent**: They may guide and ensure everything goes smoothly. If they are not attending, ask them if they can be sure they are available if you have a question.
  - ○ **Lender's representative**: Ensures all loan documents are accurate. (Rarely attend in person but normally just a phone call away)

What Documents Will You Sign?

Here is a preview of some key documents you will encounter:

- **Promissory Note**: Your written promise to repay the mortgage loan.
- **Deed of Trust or Mortgage**: Gives the lender rights to the property if you default.
- **Deed:** The legal document that transfers property ownership from the seller to you. While you hold the deed and are the owner of the property, your lender retains a lien on the property until the promissory note (often thought of as the mortgage) is fully paid.

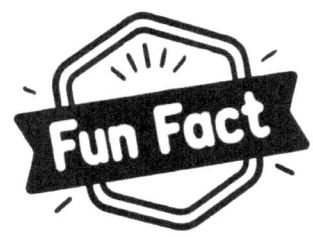

Fun Fact: The stack of papers you sign on the closing day could easily weigh a pound, do not worry, your hand will recover!

Helpful Hint: Take Your Time! Review each document carefully, verify all number amounts, and ask questions if anything is unclear. Doing so after you sign is too late. Understanding and confirming what you are signing is better than rushing through it.

When Do I Get My Keys?

The moment you have been waiting for, getting your keys, typically happens right after the closing process is complete and the transaction is funded. Once all documents are signed and the lender has wired the funds to the appropriate party, the title company or seller, the title company, or the closing attorney will give the green light to release the keys. In most cases, you will get them immediately at the closing table, but it may take a few hours or days in others. If the seller requested a post-closing possession agreement, you might have to wait a little longer. Always confirm the timeline with your agent to avoid surprises!

Avoiding Last-Minute Surprises

To keep everything on track, avoid these common pitfalls:

- **No major financial changes**: Do not apply for new credit, change jobs, or make big purchases before closing. If this is unavoidable, talk it through with your lender PRIOR to making any changes, as you do not want it to cause your loan to be turned down and you will be unable to close on your home.

- **Stay in touch**: Be proactive and keep open communication with your lender, real estate agent, and closing agent.

- **Confirm logistics**: Double-check the time, date, and location of your closing. Also, confirm the amount needed for closing costs.

After Closing:

Welcome to Homeownership!

Once the documents are signed and the funds are transferred, you will receive the keys to your new home! Here is what to do next:

1. Change the Locks: Have the locks rekeyed for added security.

2. Set Up Utilities: Contact utility companies and transfer the accounts to your name.

3. Store Closing Documents Safely: Keep copies of all closing documents, both digitally and hard paper, for future reference, especially for tax purposes.

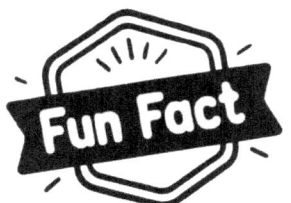 **Fun Fact**: Some buyers take a 'closing day selfie' with their keys—it is a fun way to celebrate and remember the big moment!

Chapter 11 Key Takeaways

- **Prepare for Closing:** Review the Closing Disclosure carefully, conduct a final walkthrough, and gather all required documents ahead of time.

- **Understand Title Insurance:** Protect yourself and your lender from potential ownership disputes by securing both lender's and owner's title policies.

- **Expect Closing Costs:** Know what costs to expect, including prepaid taxes, insurance, and other fees, and ensure you have funds ready for closing day.

- **Be Mindful of Wire Fraud:** Verify all wire transfer details directly with the title company or attorney to avoid scams.

- **Celebrate the Moment:** Closing is the culmination of your home-buying journey—relish the excitement and take that "keys-in-hand" photo!

Summary: Closing day marks the end of your home-buying journey and the beginning of homeownership. While it can feel overwhelming, being prepared ensures the process goes smoothly. This chapter covers everything from understanding title insurance and closing costs to preparing documents and avoiding wire fraud. With proper preparation and a clear understanding of what to expect, you can confidently navigate this exciting milestone. Take a deep breath, savor the moment, and get ready to create lasting memories in your new home. Congratulations!

Next, we will discuss where you buy your new home and key points that may be different.

Chapter 12

Across Borders: How Homebuying Differs in Canada, Mexico, and the U.S

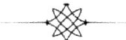

Whether you are dreaming of a beachfront retreat in Mexico, a cozy home in Canada, or navigating the U.S. market, buying a home is a significant financial step. While this book primarily focuses on the U.S. process, many of the principles apply across borders. This chapter dives into the unique aspects of buying a home in Canada and Mexico, offering insights for those living there or considering an international purchase.

We will explore key differences in financing, taxes, legal requirements, and more to help you make informed decisions, no matter where you are looking to buy. If you are based in Canada or Mexico, you will also find helpful comparisons to understand how your market operates alongside the U.S. As always, consulting local experts is crucial for navigating the specifics of your region.

1. Financing a Home

- **United States**: The U.S. offers a variety of loan options, including FHA, VA, USDA, and conventional loans. Mortgage terms often run for 15–30 years, and fixed-rate mortgages are the most popular. Lenders require a good credit score, a down payment (often 3–20%), and proof of income.

- **Canada**: Canada's mortgage system differs significantly. Most loans have shorter terms, typically 5 years, with amortization periods of 25–30 years. Fixed and variable-rate mortgages are both standard, but borrowers often renegotiate their terms at the end of each loan term. A stress test is mandatory for borrowers to ensure they can afford higher rates if they rise. Down payments start at 5% for homes under $500,000, but properties over that require at least 10% of the excess.

- **Mexico**: In Mexico, mortgages are less common for foreign buyers. Many transactions are done in cash. Financing through Mexican banks is possible, but terms are shorter (10–20 years), and interest rates are often higher than in the U.S. Foreign buyers may find it easier to obtain financing through specialized international lenders.

2. Taxes and Fees

- **United States**: Property taxes are paid annually and vary significantly by state and local jurisdiction. Closing costs typically range from 2–5% of the purchase price, including fees for title insurance, inspections, and lender services.

- **Canada**: Property taxes are also paid annually and are calculated based on the municipality. Buyers pay a land transfer tax, which varies by province, and some regions offer rebates for first-time buyers. Closing costs are lower than in the U.S., usually around 1.5–4% of the home price.

- **Mexico**: Property taxes (predial) are lower than the U.S. and Canada. Buyers must pay a transfer tax and notary fees totaling 4–6% of the purchase price. Foreign buyers may also incur additional costs for establishing a bank trust (fideicomiso) if purchasing in restricted zones like coastal or border areas.

3. The Legal Process

- **United States**: Buyers rely heavily on real estate agents and attorneys to navigate contracts, inspections, and contingencies. Title insurance protects buyers from disputes over property ownership.

- **Canada**: Real estate transactions often involve agents but do not typically require lawyers, except in some provinces. Buyers must research to ensure the property has a clear title, but title insurance is less common.

- **Mexico**: Foreign buyers must use a notary public (*notario público*), a government-appointed official who ensures the legality of the transaction. Coastal and border properties require foreign buyers to establish a bank trust (*fideicomiso*) for ownership. Buyers should hire a qualified real estate attorney to ensure the process is handled correctly.

4. Property Types

- **United States**: Buyers can choose from a wide range of properties, including single-family homes, condos, and townhouses.

"COMING HOME IS ONE OF THE MOST BEAUTIFUL THINGS."

– ANDRÉ RIEU

Home Sweet Home

- **Canada**: The market is dominated by condos in urban areas, with single-family homes being more common in suburban or rural regions.

- **Mexico**: Mexico offers a mix of traditional homes, beachfront properties, and luxury developments, with many options for expatriates and retirees.

5. Home Inspections

- **United States**: Home inspections are a critical part of the process and are often required before closing. Depending on the seller and market, buyers may be able to negotiate repairs or price reductions based on inspection findings.
- **Canada**: Home inspections are also common, especially in competitive markets, but they are not always required.
- **Mexico**: Home inspections are less formalized and may not be standard practice. Buyers should hire independent inspectors to assess the property.

6. Seller Disclosures: What Buyers Should Know

Seller disclosures are a vital part of the home buying process, but their requirements differ by country:

- **United States**: Most states require sellers to provide a disclosure outlining known issues with the property, such as structural defects, past water damage, or other material problems. These disclosures give buyers a clearer understanding of the home's condition before making an offer. However, requirements vary by state, and buyers should consult their agent to understand local laws.
- **Canada**: While some provinces have mandatory seller disclosure forms, others do not. In areas where disclosures are not required, buyers may need to rely more heavily on inspections to uncover potential issues.

- **Mexico**: Seller disclosures are not commonly required, and it is up to the buyer to perform thorough due diligence. Hiring a local real estate attorney and independent inspector is essential to identify any hidden problems with the property.

7. Cultural and Practical Considerations

- **Language**: In Mexico, many transactions require fluency in Spanish or the help of a translator. In Canada, the two predominant languages are English and French.

- **Healthcare and Amenities**: Buyers in Canada and Mexico may prioritize proximity to healthcare, particularly retirees.

- **Climate and Construction**: In Mexico, homes are often built with concrete for durability in heat, while Canadian homes prioritize insulation for colder climates.

8. Additional Considerations

- **Currency Exchange Considerations** (For Mexico Buyers): For buyers purchasing property in Mexico, fluctuating exchange rates can significantly impact the final cost. Adding a note about considering currency exchange rates and working with a trusted financial institution for secure and cost-effective currency conversion could be valuable.

- **Tax Implications for Foreign Buyers:** This chapter briefly mentions taxes and fees, but adding a note about tax implications for foreign buyers (e.g., capital gains taxes when selling, annual reporting requirements, or ownership taxes for non-residents) could prevent surprises. For example:

- In Mexico, foreign buyers may face additional taxes when selling property, such as the ISR tax (capital gains tax).

- U.S. citizens buying abroad may have to report property sales to the IRS, even if the transaction occurs in another country.

- Homeowner Insurance in Different Markets: Insurance is not explicitly covered, yet it is critical for protecting investments:

  - **United States**: Homeowners insurance is usually required by lenders, and buyers should ensure they understand flood, earthquake, or hurricane coverage based on location.

  - **Canada**: Insurance policies may vary depending on the province, particularly in areas prone to natural disasters like wildfires or flooding.

  - **Mexico**: Property insurance is less common but advisable, particularly for beachfront homes or areas prone to hurricanes. Buyers should research local providers or work with their attorneys for recommendations.

- **Financing for Foreign Buyers:** Navigating financing as a foreign buyer can feel like uncharted territory, but there are several options to explore:

  - **Obtaining Loans in Mexico:** Some Mexican banks and international lenders offer financing programs specifically for non-residents. These typically require larger down payments (often 30–50%) and additional documentation, such as proof of income and a valid passport. Partnering with a bilingual loan officer or real estate attorney can simplify the process.

- ○ **Leveraging Home Equity Abroad:** If you own property in the U.S. or Canada, you can use a home equity loan or line of credit to fund your purchase in Mexico. This option often provides more favorable terms than local financing. However, it's essential to account for exchange rate fluctuations and potential risks to your existing property.

- ○ **Cash Purchases:** Many buyers choose to bypass financing entirely by paying in cash, reducing transaction times, and avoiding loan restrictions. For this approach, working with a trusted financial institution for secure currency exchange is critical.

Whichever option you choose, consulting with cross-border financial specialists or international mortgage brokers can help you navigate the complexities and find the best fit for your needs.

- **Zoning and Land Use Restrictions:** This topic is especially critical in Mexico, where zoning and land use can differ dramatically. Buyers should be aware of:
  - ○ Restrictions on building near certain areas (e.g., archaeological zones or ecological reserves).
  - ○ Regulations that could impact future renovations or expansions.

Chapter 12 Key Takeaways:

- **Understand Regional Differences:** Home-buying processes vary significantly between the U.S., Canada, and Mexico, with unique norms for financing, taxes, and legal requirements.

- **Financing Options Vary:**

    - U.S.: Offers long-term mortgages with diverse loan types.

    - Canada: Features shorter loan terms with mandatory stress tests.

    - Mexico: Financing is limited, with many transactions requiring cash or international lenders.

- **Legal Processes Differ:**

    - U.S.: Relies heavily on title insurance and agents.

    - Canada: Lawyers are optional in most provinces, but title research is crucial.

    - Mexico: Involves notary publics, bank trusts for foreigners, and additional steps for compliance.

- **Due Diligence is Key:** Seller disclosures are not universally required, particularly in Mexico, so thorough inspections and professional guidance are essential.

- **Taxes and Fees:** Be aware of property taxes, transfer taxes, and other fees specific to each country.

- **Plan for Insurance:** Homeowner insurance varies by region, with unique considerations for natural disasters or location-specific risks.

Summary: Chapter 12 provides an insightful comparison of the home-buying process in the U.S., Canada, and Mexico, highlighting the unique challenges and requirements of each country. From understanding financing options and legal differences to planning for taxes, fees, and cultural factors, this chapter equips you with essential knowledge for cross-border transactions. Whether you are purchasing a beachfront property in Mexico, a cozy home in Canada, or navigating the U.S. market, the principles of research, professional guidance, and preparation remain universal. Armed with these insights, you will be better prepared to navigate the complexities of international homebuying. Congratulations on broadening your horizons!

Next, we will uncover essential tools to help you on your path to homeownership.

Chapter 13

Homebuyer's Toolkit: Essential Tools & Websites for First-Time Buyers

In today's digital age, a wealth of tools, such as apps and websites, can make your home-buying journey easier. Whether you are calculating your budget, exploring neighborhoods, or comparing mortgage rates, the right resources can save you time, money, and stress. Let's explore some of the best tools available to help you make informed decisions.

1. Best Mortgage Calculators: A **mortgage calculator** is one of the most essential tools for any homebuyer. It helps you estimate monthly payments based on factors like loan amount, interest rate, and term.

- **Bankrate's Mortgage Calculator**

  Offers a clear breakdown of monthly payments, including principal, interest, taxes, and insurance (PITI).Website: https://www.bankrate.com/mortgage-calculators/

- **Zillow Mortgage Calculator**

  Includes additional tools for affordability and refinancing. Website: https://www.zillow.com/mortgage-calculator/

- **NerdWallet's Mortgage Calculator**

  Provides options for comparing different loan types and estimating closing costs.

  Website:https://www.nerdwallet.com/mortgages/mortgage-calculator

- **MortgageCalculator.org**

  Helps you understand what your budget can buy in today's market.

  - Website: https://www.mortgagecalculator.org/

Helpful Hint: Play around with the numbers to see how down payment, loan term, or interest rate changes affect your monthly payment. Remember that your total house payment typically includes PITI (principle, interest, taxes, and insurance).

2. Best Credit Monitoring and Reporting Sites: Your credit score plays a major role in qualifying for a mortgage and securing a good interest rate. Stay on top of it with these tools:

- **MyFico**: Provides credit score monitoring for a fee, offering alerts about changes and personalized strategies to improve your scores. It allows you to view all three merged credit bureau reports in one place.

  - Website: https://www.myfico.com
- **Experian, TransUnion, and Equifax**: These credit bureaus provide a free credit report once a year and ongoing credit tracking services.

  - Experian: https://www.experian.com
  - TransUnion: https://www.transunion.com
  - Equifax: https://www.equifax.com
- **AnnualCreditReport.com**: The official site to get your free annual credit reports from all three bureaus in one place.

○ Website: https://www.annualcreditreport.com

Tip: Monitor your credit regularly to catch errors or changes that could impact your mortgage approval.

3. Best Sites for Down Payment Assistance Programs: Many first-time buyers are eligible for down payment assistance, but finding the right program can be challenging.

- **DownPaymentResource.com**
  Helps you find programs based on your location and eligibility.
  Website: https://www.downpaymentresource.com/

- **The Federal Housing Administration (HUD.gov)**

  Offers information about state and local programs for first-time buyers.

  Website: https://www.hud.gov/topics/buying_a_home

- **NeighborWorks America**

  A nonprofit organization that provides education and assistance for buyers, including down payment resources.

  Website: https://www.neighborworks.org/

4. Best Neighborhood Research Sites: The neighborhood can be just as important as the house itself. These tools help you evaluate schools, crime rates, amenities, and commute times.

- **GreatSchools.org**: Provides detailed school ratings and reviews.

- Website: https://www.greatschools.org

- **NeighborhoodScout.com**: Offers detailed information on crime rates, income levels, housing trends, and demographic data for neighborhoods across the U.S.

  - Website: https://www.neighborhoodscout.com

- **WalkScore.com**: Measures how walkable a neighborhood is, along with nearby amenities and public transit options.

  - Website: https://www.walkscore.com

Helpful Hint: Take a virtual "walk" through potential neighborhoods using Google Street View to get a feel for the area. Also, many homes for sale have virtual tours on ads as well, so explore and enjoy. It is a good way to preview a house to see if it makes the list of what you want to see in person.

5. Top Real Estate Websites & Apps: Having access to home listings and mortgage tools on your phone can make the home search more convenient.

- **Google Street View:** Explore neighborhoods virtually with panoramic views.

  - Android: https://play.google.com/store/apps/details?id=com.google.android.street

  - iOS: https://apps.apple.com/app/google-street-view/id904418768

- **Zillow:** Browse real estate listings with virtual tours.

  - Website: https://www.zillow.com

  - Android: https://play.google.com/store/apps/details?id=com.zillow.android.zillowmap

- iOS: https://apps.apple.com/app/zillow-real-estate-rentals/id310738695
- **Realtor.com:** Access property listings with immersive virtual tours.
  - Website: https://www.realtor.com
  - Android: https://play.google.com/store/apps/details?id=com.move.realtor
  - iOS: https://apps.apple.com/app/realtor-com-real-estate/id336698281
- **Redfin:** Find homes for sale with virtual tour options.
  - Website: https://www.redfin.com
  - Android: https://play.google.com/store/apps/details?id=com.redfin.android
  - iOS: https://apps.apple.com/app/redfin-real-estate/id327962480
- **Trulia:** Discover homes and neighborhoods with virtual tours.
  - Website: https://www.trulia.com
  - Android: https://play.google.com/store/apps/details?id=com.trulia.android
  - iOS: https://apps.apple.com/app/trulia-real-estate-find-homes/id288487321
- **HomeSnap:** Search for homes, connect with agents, and view virtual tours.
  - Website: https://www.homesnap.com

- Android:
  https://play.google.com/store/apps/details?id=com.homesnap

- iOS: https://apps.apple.com/app/homesnap-real-estate-search/id301303058

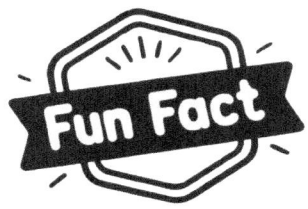 **Fun Fact**: Some apps, like Homesnap, can even show you the last sale price and property tax info with a quick photo of the house!

6. **Best Home Inspector Search Tools:** Finding a trustworthy home inspector is crucial for identifying potential issues before you buy.

- **American Society of Home Inspectors (ASHI.org)**
  - Offers a directory of certified home inspectors by area.
  - Website: https://www.homeinspector.org/
- **HomeAdvisor.com**
  - Allows you to search for highly rated inspectors in your location, with reviews from other buyers.
  - Website: https://www.homeadvisor.com/

7. **Best Home Insurance Comparison Sites:** You will need homeowners insurance before closing. Use these tools to find the best rates and coverage.

- **Policy genius**
  - ○ Offers side-by-side comparisons of multiple insurance providers.
  - ○ Website: https://www.policygenius.com/
- **The Zebra**
  - ○ Compares rates from over 100 insurers to find the best policy for your new home.
  - ○ Website: https://www.thezebra.com/

Helpful Hint: Get insurance quotes early in the process, as this will also be part of your closing costs.

8. Best Closing Cost Calculators: Closing costs can be a surprise if you are not prepared. Use these tools to estimate your costs ahead of time. This may get you a ballpark; however, to get a true estimate, get in touch with your lender.

- **Smart Asset's Closing Cost Calculator**

  - ○ Offers a detailed estimate based on home price, down payment, and location.

  - ○ Website: https://smartasset.com/mortgage/closing-costs

- **Bankrate's Closing Cost Calculator**

  Helps you understand the full cost breakdown of buying a home.

  Website: https://www.bankrate.com/mortgages/closing-cost-calculator/

Chapter 13 Key Takeaways:

- **Mortgage Calculators Are Essential:** Tools like Bankrate and NerdWallet can help estimate monthly payments and budget accurately.

- **Monitor Your Credit:** Use platforms like AnnualCreditReport.com and MyFico to track your credit score and address errors promptly.

- **Explore Down Payment Assistance:** Websites like DownPaymentResource.com and HUD.gov can connect you to programs for financial support.

- **Research Neighborhoods:** Platforms like GreatSchools.org and WalkScore.com provide valuable insights into schools, crime rates, and amenities.

- **Use Real Estate Apps:** Zillow, Redfin, and Realtor.com to make searching for homes and viewing virtual tours convenient and accessible.

Summary: This chapter equips you with a "homebuyer's toolkit" of essential digital resources to simplify every step of your journey. From mortgage calculators and credit monitoring tools to neighborhood research and real estate apps, these platforms empower you with the knowledge needed to make informed decisions. Whether calculating costs, exploring potential areas, or comparing down payment assistance programs, these tools save time, reduce stress, and boost confidence. With the right apps and websites at your fingertips, you are well-prepared to navigate the path to homeownership.

Building on what we've covered, let's move to some final thoughts and summing up what we have learned.

Final Thoughts: Your Home Sweet Home Journey

Congratulations! Reaching the end of this guide means you are now armed with the knowledge and tools to navigate the homeownership journey with confidence. From understanding credit and financing to finding the right home, completing the purchase, and settling into your new space, you have taken a significant step toward becoming a confident and well-prepared homeowner.

Owning a home is one of the most rewarding investments you can make. Beyond financial stability, it offers you the freedom to create a space that is uniquely yours and build a strong foundation for the future. Whether you are ready to buy now or still planning, the next step is yours. If you are not quite there yet, that is okay—start crafting your SMART (Specific, Measurable, Achievable, Relevant, and Time-bound) plan today. Taking action now ensures you are actively working toward your goal of homeownership and setting yourself up for long-term success.

Owning a Home: Your Path to Wealth, Stability, and Freedom

The benefits of homeownership extend far beyond having a place to call your own. Every mortgage payment builds equity, turning your home into a powerful wealth-building tool. Rising property values over time can further enhance this investment. Homeownership also offers financial perks like homestead exemptions, tax deductions for mortgage interest and property taxes, and the ability to lock in predictable monthly housing costs.

Beyond the financial advantages, owning a home provides stability, security, and privacy. It is a hedge against inflation and a way to stop building someone else's wealth through rent. Instead, every payment you make is an investment in your future. Your home reflects your style and values, offering creative freedom to design, renovate, and truly make it your own. Whether it is landscaping, planting a garden, or personalizing your interior, your home becomes a place of pride and a reflection of who you are.

The benefits of homeownership are undeniable: a path to wealth, a source of stability, and the freedom to create a life in a space that is entirely yours. If you have been waiting for the right moment, ask yourself, "Do I have a good reason not to start now?"

Your New Beginning: Buying a home is more than a transaction; it is a transformative journey. It is a mix of excitement, nervousness, and countless decisions—but each step brings you closer to something truly special. Whether you are just beginning to explore the idea, actively searching for your dream home, or preparing to close, every moment deserves to be celebrated.

The Power of Preparation: One of the greatest takeaways from this book is the importance of preparation. Equipped with the right information, a realistic budget, and a clear plan, you can approach each stage of the process with confidence. While preparation does not eliminate every challenge, it empowers you to navigate them wisely and turn potential roadblocks into opportunities.

The Road Ahead: The adventure does not end when you get the keys—it is just the beginning. Homeownership comes with new responsibilities, from maintaining your property to planning your finances, but it also offers the freedom to make your house a home. As you settle into your new space, remember these parting thoughts:

- Stay Curious: Keep learning about homeownership to protect and grow your investment.

- Be Patient: Not everything will go as planned, but every challenge is a chance to grow.

- Embrace Joy: Your home is more than walls and a roof—it is your sanctuary, a place for comfort, pride, and happiness.

Reflecting on Your Journey: Homeownership is a milestone worth celebrating. It is a place to build wealth, establish roots, and, most importantly, create memories. Take a moment to reflect on how far you have come and all the steps that brought you here. Each decision, each step forward, has led to this—your very own Home Sweet Home.

Welcome Home: This is a new chapter in your life, and it is filled with endless possibilities. Your home is not just a financial investment but a personal one—a foundation for dreams, laughter, and milestones yet to come.

So here is to you and your journey. May it be filled with growth, happiness, and, above all, the feeling of truly being home.

Welcome to your Home Sweet Home.

Let the memories begin!

"THERE IS SOMETHING PERMANENT, AND SOMETHING EXTREMELY PROFOUND, IN OWNING A HOME."

- KENNY GUINN

Home Sweet Home

Chapter 14

From Dreaming to Owning: Your Essential Homebuying Checklist

This checklist will guide you through the entire home-buying process, primarily in chronological order from what to do **before closing** to tasks for the **first 30 days after closing.** Remember that real estate is fluid, so your checklist might be out of sequence. Use it to stay organized, as a tool to help you ask more questions and ensure a smooth transition to homeownership.

Your Home Sweet Home Checklist: A Step-by-Step Home Buying Checklist

These lists are primarily in chronological order, but some tasks may happen out of sequence—and that is perfectly fine. It is designed to serve as a helpful reference, giving you a checklist to follow and prompting questions along the way.

Checklist: From Prequalification to Contract

- **Determine Your Budget**

  - ☐ Create your budget: Review your current finances, including income and all debts, noting payment amounts and payoff timelines. Consider how much you can comfortably afford for a house payment or whether paying off certain debts could improve your monthly cash flow. Gather your financial documents and remember to get prequalified for expert advice in creating a tailored plan for your situation.

☐ Get prequalified for a mortgage. (An initial estimate of how much you can borrow based on the basic financial information you provide.)

    ☐ Preferably via a soft pull so that it does lower your credit score. Once you decide what lender you plan to use, then they will do a hard pull.

    ☐ Ask the lender if they can share your credit report with you. If not, that is okay. Just go online and order it yourself so you know what's on there.

☐ Set your SMART Goals (Specific, Measurable, Achievable, Relevant, and Time-bound) - with wisdom and guidance from your lender, determine whether you are ready to buy a home now, what is a realistic timeline, and what your roadmap is to get there. Also, set a realistic home price range and ask the lender what the MAX you will qualify for (and then you can set your ideal limits as long as you stay under this)

- **Check Your Credit Score**

  ☐ Obtain your credit report.

  ☐ Dispute any errors and improve your score if needed.

- **Down Payment & Closing Costs**

  ☐ Do you have enough liquid cash ready to go?

  ☐ If not, establish a savings plan with clear SMART Goals, outlining where your funds will come from and when you will reach your target.

- **Find a Real Estate Agent**
  - ☐ Interview potential agents, and if you are ready to begin house hunting, sign a buyer representation agreement. Some buyers choose to start with a real estate agent first, as the agent can recommend a trusted lender from their network.

- **Get Preapproved for a Mortgage** (This is much stronger than a prequalification. It is a more detailed process where the lender verifies your financial documents and confirms a specific loan amount.)
  - ☐ Submit the required documents to the lender.
  - ☐ Obtain a preapproval letter to strengthen your offers. (Note that a preapproval letter is much stronger than a prequalification letter.)

- **Start House Hunting**
  - ☐ Make a list of must-haves and nice-to-haves. Remember to utilize your scale of 1-10
  - ☐ Tour homes with your agent.

- **Make an Offer (or a counteroffer)**
  - ☐ Work with your agent to negotiate terms.
  - ☐ Include contingencies like inspection, financing, and appraisal.
  - ☐ Include a closing date in your offer. If the home is move-in ready, closing usually occurs within 30 to 45 days unless otherwise negotiated.
  - ☐ Define the **option period**, a timeframe (typically 7-10 days) that allows you to back out of the contract for any reason after inspections. The name for this period varies by location and may be referred to as a due diligence period, inspection

contingency, or inspection period. Be sure to ask your realtor what it is called in your area.

- [ ] Offer earnest money and option fee amounts that demonstrate your commitment.
- [ ] Clarify what is staying with the home. Typically, anything attached to the property remains, but it is always best to confirm. You can also negotiate for additional items, such as a refrigerator or outdoor grill. Keep in mind the seller might have an attached item with sentimental value that they plan to take with them. Make sure all agreements are clearly outlined in your contract to avoid misunderstandings.
- [ ] Clearly outline who covers costs like closing costs, title policy, home warranty, and any requested repairs.

- **The offer is accepted, And all parties have signed the paperwork**
    - [ ] The paperwork and typically your earnest money are sent to the title company/closing attorney/closing agent
    - [ ] Notify your lender immediately and send them a copy of your fully signed contract.

- **YAY!!!** It is time to do a happy dance. You are officially on the path to homeownership! This is an exciting milestone, and remember that the next few weeks will involve several time-sensitive tasks to keep the process moving smoothly.

Checklist: Things to Complete BEFORE Closing

- **Schedule a Home Inspection** (typically, this has a time limit in your contract, often called "Option Period," so get this completed right away)

  - ☐ Hire a licensed inspector.

  - ☐ Review the report and request/negotiate any necessary repairs.

- **Gather Required Documents**

  - ☐ Follow up with your lender, ask them what else they need, and get it to them right away.

- **Secure Homeowners Insurance**

  - ☐ Make sure coverage is scheduled to be in place by closing day.

- **Confirm Closing Details**

  - ☐ Double-check the date, time, and location of your closing appointment & add all the details to your calendar.

- **Plan Your Moving Date Wisely**

  - ☐ Decide whether to handle the move yourself or hire professional movers. Remember to avoid locking in dates too early, as closing and possession dates often shift unexpectedly.

- **Review Your Closing Disclosure** (This must be reviewed and signed a minimum of 3 days before closing)

  - ☐ Ensure all costs and terms match your expectations. Ask your lender about anything that does not make sense or looks different than you expected.

- **Prepare Closing Funds**
    - ☐ 1-3 Days before closing, arrange a **certified check or wire transfer** for closing costs and down payment. (Check with your title company for any requirements and instructions.)
    - ☐ Reminder to call and confirm with the Title Company/closing agent the wire instructions BEFORE sending the wire.
    - ☐ Confirm the wire has been received.
- **Do a Final Walkthrough**
    - ☐ 1-2 Days before closing, check that the home is in the expected condition.
- **Attend Closing**
    - ☐ Bring ID, proof of insurance, and any other documents your lender requests.
    - ☐ Review, verify, and sign closing documents.
    - ☐ Getting Keys: Funding must be completed before keys will be released. This can be a few minutes, a few hours, and sometimes even a few days.
- **Celebrate!**
    - ☐ You are officially a homeowner!

Checklist: Things to do immediately AFTER Your Closing

- **Change the Locks**
    - ☐ Have all locks, garage door openers, and security codes reprogrammed or rekeyed for added security.

- **Locate Shut-Off Valves and Circuit Breakers:**

  - ☐ Know where the main water shut-off valve and electrical circuit breaker panel are located in case of an emergency.

- **Transfer Utilities**

  - ☐ Set up accounts for electricity, water, gas, internet, and trash services. Some of these may be set up ahead of time to occur on your closing date or, rather, your moving-in date if they are not the same.

- **Update Your Address**

  - ☐ Notify the post office, banks, credit cards, insurance providers, Department of Motor Vehicles (DMV) employers, and any other relevant services at your new address.

- **Review Your Homeowners Insurance Policy**

  - ☐ Ensure it covers your home adequately as planned, and add any riders for special coverage (e.g., flood insurance, specific valuables).

- **Store Closing Documents Safely**

  - ☐ Keep all closing documents, including the deed and title, in a secure place, preferably in a fire safety box.

- **Test Safety Features**

  - ☐ Check all smoke detectors, carbon monoxide detectors, and fire extinguishers. Create a plan to check them at regular intervals as well, and set up your reminders.

  - ☐ Create a fire escape plan for your household.

Things to Complete in the First 30 Days AFTER Closing

- **Plan for Mortgage Payments**

  - ☐ Within 2 weeks from closing, confirm your mortgage payment schedule and set up autopay if desired.

- **Register Warranties**

  - ☐ For appliances, HVAC systems, and any other items that came with the house (registering may give you extended warranties)

- **Apply for Homestead Exemption**

  - ☐ If applicable in your state, this can lower your property taxes.

- **Document Your Belongings for Insurance:**

  - ☐ Take photos or videos of your valuable items and document them for insurance purposes, especially if you are upgrading furniture or appliances. Save digital copies on a USB drive and put it in your fire safety box.

- **Create a Home Maintenance Budget**

  - ☐ Set aside 1% to 2% of your home's value annually for repairs and upkeep.

- **Review Inspection Report:**

  - ☐ Review the home inspection report again to prioritize any repairs or upgrades you may want to address now that you own the home.

- **Set Up Routine Maintenance**

  - ☐ Schedule services like HVAC inspection, pest control, and gutter cleaning.

- **Organize Your Space**

  - Unpack, set up furniture, and make the space feel like *your* home.

- **Decorate with a Plan**

  - Take your time choosing paint colors, new furniture, and decor; no rush.

- **Monitor Property Tax Assessments**

  - Review your annual property assessment and consider protesting if the value seems too high. Ask your realtor about property tax deadlines and protests in your area to set reminders. Even if your taxes are paid through an escrow account, it is essential to monitor tax values and protest if necessary.

- **Connect with Neighbors**

  - To stay informed, introduce yourself and join any neighborhood groups or social media pages.

- **Create an Emergency Fund for Home Repairs**:

  - Build a separate savings account for unexpected repairs, like a broken water heater or roof leak.

- **Familiarize Yourself with Local Services**:

  - Find nearby doctors, emergency services, grocery stores, and hardware stores.

- **Evaluate Home Security**:

  - Consider installing a security system or video doorbell for added peace of mind. This can lower your insurance rates. Check with your insurance company for these types of discounts.

- **Set Financial Goals for Paying Off Your Home Faster**

    - Consider biweekly payments, making extra payments toward principal, or refinancing for a shorter term.

- **Update Your Will:**

    - If you have a will, update it to include your new property. This ensures your assets are adequately managed in case of unforeseen events. If you do not have a will, look into getting one.

- **Expert Insight for New Construction**

    - Set a calendar reminder at the 10-month mark to inspect your home and report issues before the 1-year warranty expires.

- **Other** (add your own items)

These checklists will help you confidently transition into homeownership, ensuring that you are prepared, protected, and ready to enjoy your new space.

Glossary of Terms

Here is a list of commonly used terms to help you on your new home journey.

1. **Adjustable-Rate Mortgage (ARM)**: A type of mortgage where the interest rate changes periodically based on market conditions, leading to fluctuations in monthly payments.
2. **Amortization**: The process of gradually paying off a loan over time through regular, scheduled payments. An amortization schedule breaks down each payment, showing how much goes toward reducing the loan's principal balance and how much is applied to interest.
3. **Appraisal**: An unbiased estimate of the property's market value performed by a licensed appraiser. Lenders require appraisals to ensure the home is worth the loan amount.
4. **Assessed Value**: The value assigned to a property by a local government for tax purposes.
5. **As-Is, Where-Is**: A term used in real estate transactions indicating that the property is being sold in its current condition, with no guarantees or warranties from the seller about its quality or functionality. The buyer assumes full responsibility for any repairs or issues.
6. **Closing Costs**: Expenses incurred when purchasing a home, including loan origination fees, title fees, appraisal costs, and attorney fees. Typically, it ranges between 2-5% of the loan amount.
7. **Closing Disclosure (CD)**: A document provided by the lender at least three days before closing. It outlines the final terms of your mortgage, including the loan amount, interest rate, and all associated costs, as well as the total cost of the loan over its lifetime.
8. **Comparable Sales (Comps)**: Recently sold properties similar in location, size, and features used to determine a home's market value.
9. **Contingency**: Conditions in a purchase agreement that must be met for the deal to close. Common contingencies include financing, home inspection, and appraisal.

10. **CPA**: Certified Public Accountant, also known as a Tax Advisor. It can help you understand the tax benefits and implications of a home purchase and how this might lower your taxable income.
11. **CTC (Clear to Close)**: The lender's formal approval to proceed with closing the mortgage loan. It signifies that all underwriting conditions have been satisfied, the loan file is complete, and the borrower is ready to move to the final step—signing the closing documents and officially securing the loan.
12. **Days on Market (DOM):** The number of days a property has been listed for sale.
13. **Debt-to-Income Ratio (DTI)**: A percentage comparing your total monthly debt payments to your gross monthly income. Used by lenders to determine your ability to handle additional debt.
14. **Debt Consolidation Loan**: A loan that combines multiple debts into one monthly payment, often with lower interest rates.
15. **Deed**: The legal document transferring property ownership from the seller to the buyer.
16. **Down Payment**: The amount of money paid upfront toward the purchase price of the home. Typically, 3-20% of the home's price, depending on the loan type.
17. **Earnest Money**: A deposit made by the buyer to show their serious intent to purchase the property. If the sale goes through, it is applied toward the down payment or closing costs.
18. **Equity**: The difference between the property's market value and the outstanding loan balance.
19. **Escrow**: A third-party service that holds funds and documents until all conditions of a real estate transaction are met. (Also called the title company, closing agent, or closing attorney.)
20. **Escrow Account**: A special account managed by your lender to hold funds for property taxes and homeowners insurance.
21. **Escrow Shortage**: Occurs when there are not enough funds in an escrow account to pay taxes or insurance.

22. **FHA Loan**: A government-backed loan with more lenient credit and down payment requirements.
23. **Fixed-Rate Mortgage**: A mortgage with an interest rate that remains the same for the entire loan term, leading to consistent monthly payments.
24. **Foundation Settlement**: The gradual sinking of a home's foundation, which may require repairs.
25. **Homestead Exemption**: A tax benefit that lowers property taxes for homeowners using the property as their primary residence.
26. **Home Inspection**: An examination of the property's condition by a licensed professional to identify any potential issues or repairs needed.
27. **Homeowners Association (HOA)**: An organization that manages a community or condominium. It enforces rules and may collect fees for property upkeep.
28. **Lien**: A legal claim against a property, often due to unpaid debts like a mortgage or tax bill.
29. **Loan Estimate (LE)**: A document provided by the lender that outlines the terms of a mortgage, including the interest rate, monthly payment, and closing costs.
30. **Loan Officer**: Your main point of contact who helps you apply for a loan, explains options, and gathers initial documents.
31. **Loan Processor**: Collects and organizes your financial documents to prepare the loan file for underwriting.
32. **Loan-to-Value (LTV)**: A financial ratio comparing the loan amount to the property's value, expressed as a percentage. It helps lenders assess risk.
33. **Mortgage Insurance**: Insurance that protects the lender if the borrower defaults on the loan. Required for loans with down payments of less than 20%.
34. **Offer**: A formal proposal by a buyer to purchase a property at a specified price. If accepted by the seller, it becomes a binding agreement.
35. **Origination Fee**: A fee charged by a lender for processing a new loan application.
36. **PITI**: Stands for Principal, Interest, Taxes, and Insurance, the components of a typical monthly mortgage payment.

37. **Points (Discount Points)**: Optional upfront fees are paid to lower your mortgage interest rate.
38. **Pre-Approval**: Written confirmation from a lender committing to provide a mortgage for a specified amount after thoroughly reviewing the borrower's financial details. This demonstrates to sellers that the buyer is serious and financially prepared.
39. **Prepayment Penalty:** A fee charged if you pay off your mortgage early. (This would be rare in a typical home loan but common in commercial and investor loans.)
40. **Prequalified**: An initial estimate of your borrowing potential based on self-reported financial details. No formal document review by the lender. Helps establish a price range but does not guarantee loan approval.
41. **Price Per Square Foot:** A metric used to compare property values, calculated by dividing the sale price by the property's square footage.
42. **Principal**: The original amount of money borrowed in a mortgage, excluding interest. Over time, mortgage payments reduce the principal balance.
43. **Property Taxes**: Taxes local governments impose on property owners, typically based on the home's value. These are often included in monthly mortgage payments via an escrow account.
44. **Rapid Re-score: Fix It Fast, Score It Faster:** Used by Mortgage lenders and brokers to quickly recalculates your credit score after corrections or payments, ideal for tight deadlines.
45. **Seller Disclosure:** A document that outlines known issues with the property, required in many states.
46. **Title**: A legal document that proves ownership of a property. A clear title is required for a sale to proceed.
47. **Title Insurance**: Insurance that protects the buyer and lender against losses from title defects or disputes.
48. **VA Loan**: A mortgage option for veterans, active-duty service members, and their families, offering favorable terms.
49. **Walk-Through**: A final inspection of the home before closing allows the buyer to ensure any agreed-upon

repairs are completed and that the house is in the expected condition.

50. **Zestimate**: Zillow's estimated market value of a home is often used as a reference during the buying process. (Accuracy may vary by area, so always have your real estate agent also run a comparable market analysis called CMA.)

Glossary of Industry Terms Specific to New Home Construction

Here is a glossary of industry terms commonly used in new home construction to help you better understand the process and communicate effectively with builders, contractors, and inspectors.

1. **Allowance:** A set amount of money included in the construction budget for specific items, such as fixtures or appliances, where exact costs may not be known in advance. Homeowners can choose products within this budget or pay extra for upgrades.

2. **As-Built Drawings:** Drawings or plans that show the house as it was actually constructed, including any changes made during construction that differ from the original plans.

3. **Architectural Plans:** Detailed drawings created by an architect that outline the design and specifications for a home, including floor plans, elevations, and structural details.

4. **Blueprint:** Detailed technical drawings used by builders and contractors that outline the specifications, layout, and dimensions of the house.

5. **Builder's Warranty:** A warranty provided by the builder covering certain defects or issues in the home, typically for a set period after construction is completed, usually one to ten years.

6. **Building Code:** Local or national standards that regulate construction practices to ensure buildings are safe and structurally sound.

7. **Building Envelope:** The physical barrier between the interior and exterior of a building, including walls, windows, doors, roof, and foundation. It controls temperature, moisture, and airflow.

8. **Certificate of Occupancy (CO):** A legal document issued by the local government certifying that the home complies with building codes and is safe for occupancy.

9. **Closing Costs:** Fees associated with finalizing the home purchase, including loan processing fees, title insurance, property taxes, and other administrative expenses.

10. **Custom Build:** A home that is designed and built specifically for the homeowner, often allowing for complete customization of materials, floor plans, and finishes.

11. **Crawl Space:** A shallow space beneath the house that allows access to plumbing, electrical wiring, and mechanical systems, usually found in homes without basements or slab foundations.

12. **Drywall:** Also known as gypsum board, drywall is a material used to create the interior walls and ceilings of a home. It is installed after the framing and electrical wiring.

13. **Draw:** A payment made to a builder or contractor at specific milestones during the construction process, usually tied to the completion of certain project phases.

14. **Design-Build:** A construction approach where the design and construction services are provided by the same company or contractor, streamlining the process for the homeowner.

15. **Easement:** A legal right granted to a third party to use a portion of your property for specific purposes, such as utility lines, sidewalks, or road access.

16. **Elevation:** A drawing that shows the exterior sides of the house, including details of windows, doors, and rooflines.

17. **Energy Efficiency Rating (HERS):** The Home Energy Rating System **(HERS)** measures a home's energy efficiency, with lower scores indicating better efficiency. A score of 100 represents a standard new home (based on 2006 energy efficiency standards). A score of 0 means the house is a net-zero energy, producing as much energy as it uses. If a home has a HERS score of 50, then it is 50% more energy-efficient than a standard new home.

18. **Erosion Control**: Measures to prevent soil erosion during and after construction.

19. **Footings:** The base of a house's foundation, typically made of concrete, which spreads the weight of the building to prevent settling or shifting.

20. **Framing:** The wooden or steel skeleton of the house that supports the walls, roof, and floors. It is the structural core of the home.

21. **Finish Carpentry:** The final stage of carpentry work in the home, including installing trim, molding, doors, and cabinetry.

22. **General Contractor (GC):** The person or company responsible for overseeing the entire construction project, including hiring subcontractors, scheduling, and ensuring the work is completed to code.

23. **Grade:** The slope or level of the land on which the house is built. Proper grading ensures water flows away from the foundation to prevent flooding or moisture damage.

24. **Hard Costs:** Direct construction costs such as materials, labor, and equipment, as opposed to soft costs like permits, taxes, and fees.

25. **Heating, Ventilation, and Air Conditioning (HVAC).** Refers to the systems that regulate temperature, airflow, and overall climate inside a home.

26. **Inspection:** A formal review conducted by a certified inspector to ensure that construction complies with local building codes and industry standards. Inspections

typically occur at key construction phases, such as framing, plumbing, electrical, and final.

27. **Insulation:** Materials used in the walls, attic, and floors to reduce heat loss or gain, improving the home's energy efficiency and comfort.

28. **Joists:** Horizontal beams that support the floors and ceilings in a house. They are typically made of wood or steel.

29. **Load-Bearing Wall:** A wall that supports the structure's weight above it. Removing or altering a load-bearing wall requires careful planning and often the addition of beams for support.

30. **Lot:** The plot of land on which the home is built.

31. **Mechanicals:** Refers to the heating, cooling, plumbing, and electrical systems of the home.

32. **Millwork:** Any type of woodwork or building materials produced in a mill, such as doors, molding, trim, and cabinetry.

33. **Punch List:** A list of items that still need to be completed or repaired before the home is considered fully finished. It is typically created during the final walk-through of the house.

34. **Permit:** An official document issued by the local government allowing construction work to proceed. It ensures that the project meets local building and safety codes.

35. **R-Value:** A measure of insulation's ability to resist heat flow. The higher the R-value, the better the insulation's effectiveness.

36. **Rough-In:** The initial phase of construction where framing, plumbing, electrical wiring, and ductwork are installed, but before drywall or finishes are added.

37. **Soft Costs:** Indirect expenses in a construction project, such as permits, architectural fees, legal fees, and financing charges.

38. **Subcontractor:** A specialized worker or company hired by the general contractor to complete a specific part of the construction project, such as electrical work, plumbing, or painting.

39. **Trim:** Decorative woodwork or moldings installed around doors, windows, and along the edges of floors and ceilings for aesthetic purposes.

40. **Underlayment:** A material placed under flooring, such as tile or hardwood, to provide a smooth surface, noise reduction, or moisture barrier.

41. **Variance:** A legal exception to zoning rules that allows a home to be built in a way that would normally violate local regulations, such as building closer to the property line.

42. **Walk-Through:** A final inspection where the homeowner and builder review the home for unfinished or unsatisfactory work. This typically occurs just before closing.

43. **Zoning:** Regulations set by local governments that determine how land can be used, such as residential, commercial, or industrial. It also governs building heights, lot sizes, and setbacks from the street.

Conclusion:

These terms are essential for navigating the construction process of a new home. Knowing this terminology will help you understand what your builder is talking about and assist you in making informed decisions throughout the project.

"NINETY PERCENT OF ALL MILLIONAIRES BECOME SO THROUGH OWNING REAL ESTATE."

- ANDREW CARNEGIE

Home Sweet Home

References & Citations

- Gaylene Rogers Lonergan, Lonergan Law Firm PLLC, Dallas, Texas www.lonerganlaw.com
- Alfonso Guzman Sr Loan Officer, NMLS 1191940, Ignite Loan Partners, Mortgage Broker www.igniteloanpartners.com
- Seth & Jocelyn Mills, Texas Sold Em Realty Group https://texassoldem.com/
- Brandy Olaniyan, Real Estate Agent, Brandy O Realty Group https://www.instagram.com/brandyorealtor
- Federal Reserve. (n.d.). *Consumer price index and inflation data*. Retrieved from https://www.federalreserve.gov/
- Mortgage Bankers Association. (n.d.). *Mortgage interest trends*. Retrieved from https://www.mba.org/
- National Association of Realtors. (n.d.). *Housing market data and statistics*. Retrieved from https://www.nar.realtor/
- U.S. Department of Housing and Urban Development. (n.d.). *FHA loan information*. Retrieved from https://www.hud.gov/
- U.S. Department of Veterans Affairs. (n.d.). *VA home loans*. Retrieved from https://www.va.gov/
- U.S. Department of Agriculture. (n.d.). *USDA rural housing programs*. Retrieved from https://www.rd.usda.gov/
- FICO. (n.d.). *Understanding your credit score*. Retrieved from https://www.myfico.com/
- Zillow. (n.d.). *Research tools and data insights*. Retrieved from https://www.zillow.com/research/
- Realtor.com. (n.d.). *Real estate trends and market analysis*. Retrieved from https://www.realtor.com/research
- Internal Revenue Service. (n.d.). *Tax information for homeowners*. Retrieved from https://www.irs.gov/

Your Next Step:
Unlock Your Free Home-Buying Tools!

Congratulations on completing *Home Sweet Home: A Step-by-Step Guide for First-Time Home Buyers!* Your journey to homeownership doesn't end here; it is just beginning.

We've prepared exclusive, customizable tools to make your journey even smoother:

Special Gifts to Simplify Homeownership!

- Personalized home-buying checklists.
- Customizable House Hunting scale of 1-10 Checklist.
- Handy charts & Glossary of Terms
- **BONUS GIFT**: From Rents to Riches - 10 Ways Owning a Home Creates Wealth!

Scan the QR Code Below or Click the Link!

www.urmspublishing.com/home-sweet-home-bonus

www.urmspublishing.com/home-sweet-home-bonus

Be a Part of Someone Else's Homeownership Story!

Thank you for joining me on this journey through *Home Sweet Home*! If this book helped clarify your homeownership path, your review could do the same for someone else.
It is a small action with a **BIG** impact.

Making a difference is *easy!*

Just scan the QR code or click the link below to share your review:

https://a.co/d/62i4TOQ

Your effort to contribute to the conversation and share good vibes is deeply appreciated.
Thank you for helping transform lives!

Thanks again, Sally Street

URMS Publishing: Inspired by Sunshine

Inspired by the song **You Are My Sunshine**, a melody deeply woven into our family's story, URMS Publishing is dedicated to spreading light through knowledge, wisdom, and practical advice, creating ripples of kindness and empowerment for today and future generations.

Love books? Become part of our story!
By joining our "VIP Readers Team", you will enjoy:

- **FREE Books:** Receive exclusive eBooks or special releases as a thank-you for joining.
- **Beta Reader Opportunity:** Help review and shape new books before they are published.
- **First-to-Know Alerts:** Be informed about special sales, events, and promotions ahead of the general public.
- **Exclusive Loyalty Rewards:** Earn points or credits for participating in activities or sharing feedback.

Join today to get behind-the-scenes access
and early VIP reader privileges.

Join here to get early Access!

urmspublishing.com/connect

"OWNING A HOME ISN'T JUST AN INVESTMENT IN REAL ESTATE—IT'S AN INVESTMENT IN YOURSELF, YOUR FUTURE, AND THE LIFE YOU WANT TO BUILD."

- SALLY STREET

Home Sweet Home

Mastering Credit Repair

DIY Guide Featuring Insider Secrets, Pro Advice to Fix Bad Credit, Easily Boost Your Score, and Unlock Proven Wealth Building Strategies

COMING SOON

SALLY STREET

We've got more Sunshine coming your way!

Visit our official book page to check out upcoming releases, grab free eBooks during promos, or join our Early Reader VIP Team!

www.urmspublishing.com/books

www.urmspublishing.com

.

www.ingramcontent.com/pod-product-compliance
Lightning Source LLC
Chambersburg PA
CBHW061740120626
46550CB00005B/1838